AN IN'.

MW00479857

ASPERGER'S SYNDROME

A journey from diagnosis to discovery, exploring real life stories and practical solutions

By Mark Blakey
With contributing articles from: Cynthia Kim,
Carol Edwards, Bushy Van Eck, Clayton Ulrich
Nuckelt, Paddy Joe Moran, Sang H. Kim, Robert
Laing and Nancy Dechter.

The authors of this book have written this as a guide containing helpful suggestions. This book is not intended as a substitute for professional medical advice. The reader should regularly consult a physician in matters relating to his/her health and particularly with respect to any symptoms that may require diagnosis or medical attention.

Certain links within the book are affiliate links which means if a product is purchased through the link the author will receive a commission. This is administered through Amazon Services LLC Associates Program, an affiliate advertising program designed to provide a means for sites to earn advertising fees by advertising and linking AspergersTestSite to Amazon properties including, but not limited to, amazon.com.

Thank you for downloading our book

Thank you for downloading our book. We hope that it gives you some valuable insights and tools that you can use in your life.

We would be really grateful if you would review the book on Amazon.com. We do appreciate your feedback, and if you have suggestions about how this book could be improved please feel free to drop us a line at info@AspergersTestSite.com.

For more helpful information on Asperger's Syndrome you can subscribe to our newsletter at: http://www.aspergerstestsite.com/newsletter.

Table of contents

Introduction

This book was created as a beginner's guide for those who have recently discovered they have, or think they may have, Asperger's Syndrome as well as for family members who are looking for information on their family's behalf.

For me, there was no guidance available to help me on my way from self-discovery to fully understanding all aspects of the condition. While the insight that I had Asperger's was a revelation, it still took me a while to understand fully all of the different aspects of it. I always knew I was different but the moment of realization was actually quite liberating and empowering for me.

Back in early 2012 I set up the Asperger's Test Site to give an opportunity for everyone to get access to an online diagnosis. Since then, I have seen a huge influx of people getting tested and subsequently requesting more information and help. It's not possible for me to respond individually to each person but my hope is that by my writing this book, I may be able to answer most people's questions. It is comprised of a compilation of some blog content as well as new and rewritten articles created specifically for the purpose.

Many people have contributed to the site over the years and several have kindly given permission for me to include their articles within this publication. The articles range from advice to real life stories where people talk about their journeys with Asperger's.

I have observed from the number and intensity of comments, in particular on the real life stories, that many of you appreciate this because it makes you feel less alone on your journey (sadly, many people on the spectrum feel alone).

While the condition is more common in society than we think, for many of us it's rare when we come across others with Asperger's and even rarer when they are willing to share what their life experience is like.

I aim to keep both the book and the blog updated with new information as it becomes available. If you are not on our newsletter mailing list you can sign up here: http://www.aspergerstestsite.com/

newsletter.

One of the things we all yearn for is hope — hope that tomorrow will be a better day than today, hope that we can attain the things our hearts desire, such as a relationship or acceptance by others.

Regardless of whether people have Asperger's or are neurotypical/NT (a fancy word for "having a 'normal' brain"), people can find a reason to blame something or someone if they don't have the life they want. I don't believe in blaming; I believe we all can create the life that we want.

Having said that, there are positive and negative aspects to having Asperger's Syndrome. I'll be honest by saying that, for me, it is both a blessing and a curse. I know there are some radical people in the Autism community who will jump on me for saying that, but that's my personal experience.

I don't believe there is anyone with Asperger's who doesn't sometimes feel like it is a curse, wishing they were someone different or somehow 'normal'. But from my experience of what is possible, these moments become more and more fleeting if Asperger's is viewed properly.

For those of you who are fans of the popular movie "The Matrix", there is a moment when Morpheus offers pills that allow one to choose to forget everything one knows about the truth and merge back into conventional reality. Sometimes I have thought about this situation in terms of whether I would choose to be neurotypical (NT) or not if I were given that opportunity. I have come to the conclusion that I would definitely choose to have Asperger's, because it makes me who I am. It is a gift that provides the potential to comprehend situations in a unique way and unusual creativity. Knowing now what I know about visual thinking and the genius capacity that comes with it, I can honestly say my life would be boring in comparison were I neurotypical.

Sure, there are things that I don't like, difficulties that I face and situations that can seem unbearable, but, given all that, I would still choose to live with this gift.

Over the years, my focus has been to overcome the things that hold me back; the things that stop me from having the life I want.

Yes, I've had to learn many things to get to that point, but that's what I've done. I've learned to harness the 'gift' aspect of Asperger's and use it to my advantage.

From running the Asperger's Test Site over the years, it has saddened me to discover that many people have NOT been able to harness that gift. I hope to write another book in the future about harnessing one's gifts, but for now this is a sharing of more general information that will hopefully shine some light on your journey of self-discovery. The goal is acclimation to the fact that we are indeed different to from the general population.

There are many out there on the Autism spectrum who think the world should adapt to them. While I understand the perceived need for this, in terms of gaining awareness and acceptance, it isn't helpful in terms of learning to live in a world that is dominated by neurotypical people — which is our realistic goal. In order to thrive rather than just survive, we have to understand their world, because the world is mostly governed by their rules.

Let me give you an analogy in terms of foreign travel. If we go to a foreign country, far away and very different from the country with which we are familiar, we can't go and expect everyone to adjust to us because we are different. We would do far better to learn and understand their ways and their language. If we do this we can expect to have a much richer and diverse experience than we will if we expected everyone to adjust to us.

In my life I have travelled to many countries. Part of my reasoning was that I was looking for answers and seeking a meaning for my existence because from a young age I knew I was different. I searched long and hard looking for Utopia, looking for answers on all levels. The places to which I travelled were not at all easy places to be, even for an NT, but for someone with Asperger's it was an extraordinary sensory overload that I put on myself, starting at the age of 21. My journey took me initially to Turkey and then to India, Nepal and Sri Lanka. I was particularly drawn to India because it is believed by many to be one of the most spiritual countries on Earth. My search for meaning took me to that place and made me stay there for one year exploring the various aspects of spirituality.

My effort to make everyone change, in order to make my life easier, was an exercise in futility. My time in India taught me to surrender, and that to be successful in any country, in any place, we need to learn to adapt.

The same is true of Asperger's. If we get fixated on who we are and how people should treat us, we miss the full experience of living.

Having researched many historical figures who evinced that they may have been on the Autism Spectrum, I have come to understand that the greatest advancements mankind has ever made would never have been possible without the obsessive and focused minds of those on the Autism spectrum. However, I can also see that it was a sacrifice for them in many aspects of their lives. They sacrificed themselves, the capacity to get recognised, and the opportunity to have deep personal relationships.

So if, until now, you haven't believed you can have the things you want in your life, I encourage you to go for it and pursue those things. Learn the skills necessary to have the life and connections you want; it can be done!

I hope this book helps you get to where you want to be.

Enjoy!

Mark

About the Writers

Mark Blakey

Mark Blakey is the founder of the Asperger's Test Site, www.AspergersTestSite.com, which he set up following his own diagnosis with Asperger's. Responding to the needs of various questions on the site, he co-authored the book "Emotional Mastery for Adults with Asperger's" and also founded "Autism Parenting Magazine" to provide a way for parents to get answers to Autism parenting-related questions. Moving away from a successful career in Information Technology, Mark had been inspired to change career and work in the field of personal growth. Training extensively in Psychotherapy, he is now a member of the British Association of Counselling and Psychotherapy (BACP). Mark runs workshops to help groups of individuals work through emotional traumas and realise their potential as human beings.

Cynthia Kim

Cynthia Kim is the proud owner of many labels, including woman, wife, mother, writer, editor, entrepreneur and, most recently, autistic. Diagnosed with Asperger's syndrome in her early forties, she began blogging about life on the spectrum at MusingsofanAspie.com. She is the author of two books on her experiences, "Nerdy, Shy and Socially Inappropriate: A User Guide to an Asperger Life" and "I Think I Might Be Autistic: A Guide to Autism Spectrum Disorder Diagnosis and Self-Discovery for Adults." She is also a contributing writer for "Autism Parenting Magazine" and the Autism Women's Network. When she isn't writing, she can often be found running or hiking backwoods trails somewhere on the east coast of the US.

Carol Edwards

Carol Edwards is a professional CBT therapist, specialising in Asperger Syndrome and OCD. She is a mother to three children and after home-educating two of her children through secondary school, one diagnosed with Asperger's and OCD, she began her role as Asperger's adviser, giving her the opportunity to advocate for families whose children and adult dependants are in education.

Please visit Carol's page (see link below) and click 'thumbs up' to help her raise more awareness.

https://www.facebook.com/
advice.cbt4autism.asperger

Carol also runs two online programmes for kids and adults living with obsessive compulsive disorder with or without Asperger Syndrome:

www.ocdonline.net and www.ocdkidsweb.com

Bushy Van Eck

Bushy Van Eck resides in Springs, South Africa. His native language is Afrikaans but you will see his English is quite exquisite. In addition he is a member of Mensa (the largest and oldest high IQ society in the world). After 25 years of personal research, Bushy brings forth a fascinating interpretation of our universe. When there is no clear understanding of a theory, when it just cannot be explained and does not make sense, then what worth is it to humanity? And if such a theory is discovered that brings a better understanding for our existence, it is truly a gift to be shared. On this premise, Bushy pulls the curtains back on scientific theories and brings them all together to reveal a purposeful meaning to our lives.

Clayton Ulrich Nuckelt

Clayton Ulrich Nuckelt is a creative writer and promoter of the "The Ultimate Understanding of the Human Existence", a collaborative effort of Bushy Van Eck's Theory of Time. Although he has a degree in marketing and worked in the fresh produce industry for many years, he has always had a passionate desire to work in the humanitarian fields. He has held the belief that no child should ever suffer from inhuman actions and that humanity is responsible to itself. Proud husband, father of six and grandfather of three, Clayton currently resides in Indiana and was raised in Southern California, where he gained a vast amount of exposure to many different cultural and spiritual beliefs.

Paddy Joe Moran

Paddy Joe Moran is a 19-year-old blogger and co-author of two autism books. He is co-founder of ASK-PERGERS?, an on-line help and advice service, and writes regular articles for various online newspapers and magazines. Paddy Joe was diagnosed with Autism/Asperger's Syndrome aged eight, and is from the UK.

He is the author of "Helping Children with Autism Spectrum Conditions through Everyday Transitions" and "Create a Reward Plan for your Child with Asperger Syndrome". He also has a blog at https://askpergers.wordpress.com/ and can be found on Twitter and Facebook.

Sang H. Kim

Sang H. Kim, Ph.D. is a lifetime martial artist and author of books on mindfulness, motivation, fitness and martial arts. His most recent book is "Mindful Movement". He also blogs at OneMindOneBreath.com.

Robert Laing

Robert discovered he had Asperger's at the age of 20, quite by chance. His mother had been given Tony Attwood's first book and recognised within it characteristics and situations similar to those encountered by both Robert and herself as a parent.

Recently, Robert has felt moved to write about

Asperger's – both his own experience with it and also the help that is available out there to others – because there are more people both being born with it and also being diagnosed with it, retrospectively, in later life. He wishes to offer help and advice to others, just as others have done for him. Aside from Asperger's Syndrome, Robert also writes for a variety of website and print publications on subjects such as music, books and the local area in which he lives.

Nancy Dechter

Nancy Dechter graduated with a B.A. in Psychology from Chatham College and an M.A. in experimental social Psychology from the University of Texas in Austin. She studied Astrology and Tarot at Manly P. Hall's Philosophical Research Society in Los Angeles.

Darren Lambert

Darren Lambert is an autistic professional musician and entertainer who has been playing piano since age 2 and singing since he could talk. He performs an average of over 40 shows per month with his wife Kristen. They live in Conneaut, Ohio, and travel all over for their

performances. They are online at
www.DarrenLambertMusic.com.

Chapter 1 - Asperger's Syndrome

What is Asperger's Syndrome?

This is a question that seems to be asked increasingly in our modern society. From engineers and computer programmers to quantum physicists, the highly intelligent but socially awkward populations of society are eventually beginning to find answers to the question they have always been busy with — "Why am I different?".

Tragically, the people who are asking the question are often people who should have been diagnosed with the condition earlier in life, but weren't, due to failures in the health and education systems. It is only now that famous celebrities are 'coming out' that Asperger's Syndrome is now in vogue.

According to medical sources, it is listed as a developmental disorder, but there is much more to it than that. It can be described as a 'hidden disability', meaning that you cannot recognise the condition from any outward appearance[1] (although the outside appearance can provide indicators).

It is important to note the manifestation of Asperger's Syndrome does vary from person to person. The below explanations are intended to be more of a guide than an absolute.

Later on in the book we will cover how Asperger's Syndrome has been incorporated into a wider diagnostic criteria of Autism. My personal opinion is that Asperger's Syndrome is deserving of its own category because we do have different lifestyles and capabilities.

Below is the official diagnosis criteria that was used in the Diagnostic and Statistical Manual, version four (DSM-IV).

"(I) Qualitative impairment in social interaction, as manifested by at least two of the following:

(A) marked impairments in the use of multiple nonverbal behaviors such as eye-to-eye gaze, facial expression, body posture, and gestures to regulate social interaction
(B) failure to develop peer relationships appropriate to developmental level
(C) a lack of spontaneous seeking to share enjoyment, interest or achievements with other people (e.g. by a lack of showing, bringing, or pointing out objects of interest to other people)
(D) lack of social or emotional reciprocity.

(II) Restricted repetitive & stereotyped patterns of behavior, interests and activities, as manifested by at least one of the following:

(A) encompassing preoccupation with one or more stereotyped and restricted patterns of interest that is abnormal either in intensity or focus
(B) apparently inflexible adherence to specific, nonfunctional routines or rituals
(C) stereotyped and repetitive motor mannerisms (e.g. hand or finger flapping or twisting, or complex whole-body movements)

(D) persistent preoccupation with parts of objects.

(III) The disturbance causes clinically significant impairments in social, occupational, or other important areas of functioning.

(IV) There is no clinically significant general delay in language (e.g. single words used by age 2 years, communicative phrases used by age 3 years).

(V) There is no clinically significant delay in cognitive development or in the development of age-appropriate self help skills, adaptive behavior (other than in social interaction) and curiosity about the environment in childhood.

(VI) Criteria are not met for another specific Pervasive Developmental Disorder or Schizophrenia."

Asperger's Syndrome (AS) has many behavioural signifiers, including difficulties in the three main areas of social communication, social interaction and social imagination. For example, subtleties in difference in tone of voice and facial expression, jokes, sarcasm, non-literal meanings and metaphors can be misunderstood, which often manifests as a perceptible social awkwardness. This can create difficulties in maintaining conventional friendships and relationships; behaviour may sometimes appear to others as clumsy or inappropriate due to an inability to read 'between the lines' and adhere to 'unwritten' social conventions. The most notable and dysfunctional characteristic of Asperger's is a lack of demonstrative empathy, which brings with it a lack of emotional and social reciprocity.[5] This, in turn, can often lead to other problems, such as feelings of isolation or depression or a strong belief within an individual that they somehow don't 'fit in'.

Another characteristic often associated with Asperger's is a difficulty to imagine more than one possible future outcome to set events; also there's a tendency to repeat a set pattern or patterns of behaviour, leading to a narrow or limited pursuit of rigid interests, such as an interest in numbers or specific details[1]. In children, this characteristic can manifest as a difficulty to engage in "let's pretend" games, and a preference instead for games involving logic or systems; for example a child with Asperger's may avoid the dressing up box but excel at maths or logic problems.

Technically, Asperger's Syndrome is classified as a type of Autism Spectrum Disorder, but for readers of this blog and our email course you will understand that there is some debate about how similar it actually is to Autism. People with the syndrome are often highly functioning and are able to cope and succeed in the world, unlike other people on the Autism Spectrum.

Recent medical studies have actually discovered that the brains of those with Asperger's Syndrome are different to those with classic Autism. You will also be interested to know that the exact symptoms develop differently in those with Asperger's. As far as classic Autism goes, many symptoms can be identified early but with Asperger's the symptoms come around a lot later.

The brains of people with Asperger's are fundamentally wired differently. Instead of thinking in language, like most people do, one is more likely to think in pictures if one has the syndrome.

In reality, what this means is an entirely different way of thinking about the world around them, producing extremely intelligent people who, in layman's terms, can do some of the most complicated tasks and find solutions to difficult problems.

The downside, of course, is that dealing with social situations becomes very difficult. When one thinks differently to the norm, it is very difficult to identify and communicate with others. Things that most people take for granted in the communication process, such as small talk and being able to identify the body language and emotions of other people, are often challenging.

All of these skills are things that we believe can be learned, but the default position makes it very difficult.

Doctors are reluctant to make an official diagnosis due to miseducation or a preference to try and identify (and therefore treat) just the most prominent symptoms. We get many emails from people who are frustrated that their doctors won't recognise their condition.

[1] The Autism Society's website: http://www.autism.org.uk/about-autism/autism-and-asperger-syndrome-an-introduction/what-is-asperger-syndrome.aspx.

[2] Peer reviewed website kidshealth.org http://kidshealth.org/parent/medical/brain/asperger.html.

[3] Klin A. (2006). "Autism and Asperger syndrome: an overview". *Rev. Bras. Psiquiatr.* **28**(suppl. 1):S3–S11. doi:10.1590/S1516-44462006000500002. PMID 16791390.

[4] Baskin J.H., Sperber M., Price B.H. (2006). "Asperger syndrome revisited". *Rev. Neurol. Dis.* **3**(1):1–7.

[5] McPartland J., Klin A. (2006). "Asperger's syndrome". *Adolesc. Med. Clin.* **17**(3):771–788. doi:10.1016/j.admecli.2006.06.010. PMID 17030291.

Symptoms of Asperger's

Before we go into detail about the testing process for Asperger's we want to describe the symptoms that one may recognise. While the symptoms of Asperger's Syndrome do vary from person to person, you may identify with any of the following:

Inflexibility/attachment to routines

Someone with Asperger's usually prefers routines and can experience emotional upset if routines are altered.

The process of moving home or even going away for a weekend or a holiday can cause distress, as can a change of job or loss of a relationship.

It can also manifest in situations where the person is focused on a particular task and gets resentful when someone interrupts to make conversation or ask a question.

Difficulty engaging in conversation

Often people with Asperger's can have difficulty engaging in conversation as well as keeping eye contact with the person they are talking to. The conversation revolves around talking about a subject the person with AS is extremely interested in, while at the same time being unable to correctly interpret the social expressions of the person being spoken to. This often results in a failure to recognise whether the other person is interested in the topic and can lead to the person being spoken to becoming bored out of their brain. However, as social etiquette dictates that they not show it, this invariably sets up a vicious cycle, because unless the person with AS gets some concrete indication that the person is not interested, he will assume they are, and keep going.

The long-term outcome of this process is that people can tend to avoid the person with AS due to their lack of social skills.

Emotional awareness and responses

It is often said the people with AS have no emotional empathy, but I would suggest that this is a myth. In actual fact people with AS have a very strong emotional sensitivity for others.

It is true that it is often difficult for people with AS

to respond to the emotions of others in the ways neurotypical (NT) people have come to expect, but it is not for lack of sensitivity.

I believe this, in part, comes from the difficulty in processing the emotions and sensory overload that occurs as a result of exposure to others' emotions. Very often this can result in withdrawal from the other person's emotions when the individual is unable to deal with both the feelings of the other and the feelings that they are also experiencing.

This has led to the belief that people with AS are cold and not empathetic.

Repetitive rituals and behaviours (stimming)

This can express itself in the engagement of repetitive rituals, such as body movements, habits and behaviours. Examples of this include hand flapping, twirling, rocking or obscure methods of play.

Stimming is usually a result of some form of anxiety or sensory overload where the person uses such motions to self sooth and feel better. It is one of the many misunderstood aspects of Autism and Asperger's. Many times children are prevented from stimming because it is deemed out of place but often, if left to stim, children will eventually release the anxiety that is causing the stimming and stop in a more calm space. If forcibly stopped, the anxiety continues only to potentially be expressed in another form, such as the (much less socially tolerated) meltdown, or through another, later, set of stims.

Sensory sensitivity

We will cover sensory issues in more detail later in the book, but we will also list it here to give you an idea what it is.

Sensory sensitivity occurs when a person has difficulty integrating and processing the various signals that enter the body through the senses. While this is often related to sound, it can also occur with the colour, texture, smell or taste of food; or it can result in a low tolerance of noises of certain frequencies.

Impaired motor skills

Sometimes one can experience an impairment of

motor skills, such as those used in playing catch, riding a bike or tying shoelaces. Although not exclusive to AS, this can often be an effect of the disorder.

From the outside, this looks like clumsiness or laziness, but in fact it is a condition and side effect, which makes hand–eye coordination and balance very difficult. There is also an anxiety associated with this aspect of AS, due to an apprehension of being required to perform some motor-based activity.

Special interests

Those with AS tend to develop special interests. A special interest is a particular hobby or subject that the person tends to become obsessed with. Often the person knows the subject inside out and develops an intense passion for it.

I believe this is one of the reasons adults with AS often excel at areas of science, engineering and computing. A high focus on one particular area makes the person an expert in the field. The downside of this, however, is that the person will have difficulty in stepping back and taking time away from their special interest.

Repetitive behaviours

This can include odd behaviours, such as lining up objects in a row or obsessively talking about the same subject repeatedly. Obsessions about eating (which foods to eat first, which foods should/ should not be combined, etc.); methods of playing and/or certain routines are also strong indicators of this condition.

Autism vs Asperger's Syndrome

Sometimes within this book and on the Asperger's Test Site we use the words 'Autism' and 'Asperger's' interchangeably. While there is a lot of debate still as to whether Asperger's and Autism are the same, we thought that it was good to explain more at this point.

Leo Kanner was the first person to describe the nature of Autism and its symptoms almost sixty years ago. Later, Hans Asperger wrote about a condition, which was first termed 'autistic psychopathology' and is now known as Asperger's Syndrome. Though there were similarities in the two discoveries, Asperger claimed that his disorder was not a variation of the initial Autism discovery.

According to the most widely used diagnostic tool, DSM-IV-TR (Diagnostic and Statistical Manual of Mental Disorders), both disorders are classified as Pervasive Developmental Disorders. Since 1994 Asperger's Syndrome was added to the fourth edition as a separate disorder.

Today the debate continues among academic researchers but there is a growing general consensus that Autism and Asperger's Syndrome are, in fact, two independent conditions, although Asperger's Syndrome had been incorporated under the umbrella of Autism to overcome clinical confusion between the diagnoses of these syndromes.

These differences are based on the different language and cognitive challenges that those with Autism and AS face.

Communication differences

Individuals with more severe forms of autism are more likely to show symptoms of limited communication skills, both verbal and non-verbal.

Diagnostic differences

Autism can be detected early, usually at the age of five, while those with AS often remain undiagnosed until eleven years old. The late onset of complex problems with social skills explains how and why people with AS are diagnosed later than their counterparts with Autism.

Studies conducted at Monash University conclude that children with Autism portray a particular style of walking; this will be fundamental in the early diagnosis of Autism as children learn to walk before they develop social skills.

Social, motor & cognitive differences

Children with Autism have limited interest in events, items and the people in their environment. They tend to favour repeated actions. Children with AS are less likely to show delays in age-appropriate skills, such as self-help, curiosity and the ability to adapt.

Autistic children, in many instances, are characterised by having motor difficulties and tend to be preoccupied with parts of objects such as the wheels of a toy car; their limited and circumscribed interest consumes a great deal of their time. Individuals with AS are less likely to display these symptoms.

Children with Autism usually have cognitive delays from early infancy. Children with AS do not tend to show this kind of delay; they might be quite talented in numeric abilities, learning to read, and being constructive in memory games.

Similarities in social & behavioural skills

Autism and High-functioning Autism (HFA) have several common characteristics with Asperger's Syndrome (AS). AS and HFA individuals have normal cognitive abilities and do not experience any significant delay in acquiring language skills.

Individuals with Autism and Asperger's Syndrome are similar in terms of their inability to create and maintain social relationships. The verbal expression of an individual with Autism might be limited or even non-existent, although certain characteristics can also be observed in individuals with Asperger's Syndrome. Despite their developed vocabulary and normal intelligence, they are unable to socialise in an acceptable manner. Their speech is overly formal and/or too literal. During interactions with peers their behaviour is deemed socially and emotionally inappropriate; this is also true for individuals with Autism. They possess similar traits in their inability to understand non-verbal signs and gestures.

Both individuals with Autism and Asperger's Syndrome have a similar behavioural profile; hence the same treatment methods can be affective for both groups. This is why some clinicians and researchers suggest that it is inappropriate to talk about two separate conditions or different disorders. A dimensional, rather than a categorical, view of Autism and Asperger's Syndrome seems to be more reasonable.

Differences in degrees of sociability

Delays and disturbances of communication are more explicit in Autism. Individuals with Asperger's Syndrome might be able to successfully complete school or find a job, which is unlikely for individuals with Autism. People with AS will experience significant impairment in important areas of functioning; for example, social interactions or correct occupational behaviour.

Important factors in their differences

The main worry in defining Asperger's Syndrome as a lesser form of Autism is that it could imply that children with AS do not face as many difficulties as those with Autism, whereas, in fact, they can suffer far more severe anxiety disorders and depression than those with Autism.

Another important factor is that the parents of those diagnosed with Asperger's Syndrome are able to be given guidelines to assist their children to develop fulfilling social activities and a chance to explore successful career options.

Further studies

Due to deeper understanding of these disorders, such as the brain cell suppression in HFA, which is not present in those with AS, resulting in variants in diagnostic tests and subsequent treatments, sufferers of both syndromes can be diagnosed and treated with the most appropriate methods. With ongoing studies into the psychological and brain differences between these syndromes, it will aid the future development of diagnostic tools and subsequent treatments for each disorder.

Chapter 2 - The Diagnosis

Getting an Official Asperger's Syndrome Diagnosis

Here we will discuss the issues and techniques surrounding diagnosis of Asperger's Syndrome. The issue has become a bit of a minefield with many doctors and general practitioners refusing to allow people the opportunity of an official diagnosis.

Many people have already taken the <u>free online AQ Test</u>, which gives people the opportunity to get an initial insight into the degree of their autistic traits without the hassle or expense of going for a medical consultation. While it gives a good general indication as to where one is on the Autism Spectrum, it is not a substitute for an official diagnosis.

We have written this post to try and represent diagnosis perspectives from a UK and US angle; however, we are aware that the advice we give may be applicable to all countries (and states).

The landscape of diagnosis is continually changing with new legislation, changes to insurance policies etc. Some people in the US have been able to get a diagnosis with their existing insurance whilst others have not. Often people end up paying to have a diagnosis. Because things differ so much, you will need to do your own research in your place of living to determine the best course of action.

Why get an official diagnosis?

The question of whether one needs to get an official diagnosis needs to be carefully considered.

For many, it is not necessary to go through the trauma of trying to get an official diagnosis. Taking online tests, reading about symptoms and understanding the intricacies of the condition can be enough. Please bear in mind that if you choose to go down the path of official diagnosis, you may not get a correct diagnosis. Sometimes people can get misdiagnosed (for example, with mental health problems such as schizophrenia). Often, doctors identify the most prominent symptom and give a diagnosis based on that alone. For example, the impaired motor skills aspect of Asperger's is often diagnosed as dyspraxia without taking into account other symptoms that may exist alongside it.

Before the changes to the Diagnostic Statistic Manual (which we will discuss later) it was easier for people with Asperger's to get support. However, now that Asperger's is grouped together with classic Autism, there is less support for people with Asperger's. While this still differs from country (and state to state), it is important to do your own research. You will find there is more specific information about details of services in the UK and US when you begin to do your own research.

The kind of support you may be able to get is:

- Social Security Income

- Disability Allowance

- Community Care.

People with Asperger's are also entitled to disability rights, where they can request specific accommodations in their workplace.

How to get officially diagnosed with Asperger's

The first step in getting an official diagnosis is speaking with your GP (doctor). They have the capacity to make referrals to either a:

- Neuropsychologist

- Psychologist

- Psychiatrist or

- Social Worker.

Very often it is the case that GP's are not so familiar with Asperger's Syndrome, so it is important to do a bit of research before you turn up for your appointment. The National Autism Society have done a great job of putting together this information pack for GP's: www.autism.org.uk/~/media/NAS/Documents/ Working-with/Health/GPs-guide-to-adults-with-

Asperger-syndrome.ashx. It may be worth your printing this out and bringing it with you to your appointment.

Due to insurance issues or budget restrictions within the health system, it is possible that your GP may not be able to refer you — in which case you could try to connect directly with a specialist.

In the US, you can find state by state information here: http://grasp.org/page/statebystate-help.

Or if you live in the UK you can check out the British Psychological Society for a list of Psychiatrists or Neuropsychologists: http://www.bps.org.uk/psychology-public/find-psychologist/find-psychologist.

In both of these cases it is advisable to seek out someone that is familiar with, or specialises in, Asperger's Syndrome.

Please bear in mind that the way assessments are carried out are not standard. You can find more guidelines that professionals should be following at: http://www.nice.org.uk/guidance/CG142.

There are also occasional opportunities at universities and other research institutions that may be available. These are often performed for free but you would need to do your own investigation to see what is possible in your area.

Do your research

I live my life on the premise that I am responsible for it, not my parents, not the medical establishment and not the government. Given that there are disturbingly high rates of misdiagnosis in the medical system, it is important to forearmed, so you can challenge things if you feel you are being misinformed.

According to this article http://www.cbsnews.com/news/12-million-americans-misdiagnosed-each-year-study-says/ 12 million Americans are misdiagnosed every year. This amounts to 1 in 20 adult patients, and in half of the misdiagnosis cases there is the potential for severe harm.

So do your research, search the internet and go prepared for any engagement with the medical system.

Free Online Testing Resources

AQ Test

One of the most common ways people get diagnosed for Asperger's Syndrome or High-functioning Autism is by using the Autism Quotient or AQ Test.

The test was published by Simon Baron-Cohen and his colleagues at the Autism Research Centre in Cambridge, UK, in 2001.[1] The test takes into account all of the factors listed above and aims "to investigate whether adults of average intelligence have symptoms of autism or one of the other autism spectrum conditions".[2] Although not intended to be a diagnostic test,[3] it has become very popular as a tool for preliminary self-diagnosis of Asperger's,[4] and further papers have indicated that it could be used clinically to screen test for the condition (suggesting that a diagnosis of Asperger's can be ruled out for those scoring less than 26).[2]

The test itself consists of questions in a 'forced choice' format, meaning that the answer is ultimately an 'agree' or 'disagree' with a given statement. It covers the five main areas associated with the Autism Spectrum: social skills; communication skills; imagination; attention to detail; and attention switching/tolerance of change.[5] Possibly due to the popularity of the test for preliminary self-diagnosis, versions of the AQ for children[6] and adolescents[7] have also been published.

The test can be taken by anyone for free at www.AspergersTestSite.com.

We've also developed a version of the AQ Test which can be used on mobile devices; there are versions for iPhone, iPad and Android.

[1] Woodbury-Smith M.R., Robinson J., Wheelwright S., Baron-Cohen S. (2005). "Screening adults for Asperger Syndrome using the AQ: a preliminary study of its diagnostic validity in clinical practice" (PDF). *J. Autism Dev.*

Disord. **35**(3):331–335. doi:10.1007/s10803-005-3300-7. PMID 16119474. Retrieved 20/10/2010.

[2] Woodbury-Smith M.R., Robinson J., Wheelwright S., Baron-Cohen S. (2005). "Screening adults for Asperger Syndrome using the AQ: a preliminary study of its diagnostic validity in clinical practice" (PDF). *J. Autism Dev. Disord.* **35**(3):331–335. doi:10.1007/s10803-005-3300-7. PMID 16119474. Retrieved 21/10/2011.

[3] Take the AQ Test, *Embarrassing Bodies* website, Channel 4, 2011. Accessed 21/10/2011.

[4] Autism Spectrum Quotient at *Answers About Autism* website (part of *Better Your Health*), 2006.

[5] Hoekstra R.A., Bartels M., Cath D.C., Boomsma D.I. (2008). "Factor structure, reliability and criterion validity of the Autism-Spectrum Quotient (AQ): a study in Dutch population and patient groups". *J. Autism Dev. Disord.* **38**(8):1555–1566. doi:10.1007/s10803-008-0538-x. PMC 2516538.

PMID 18302013.

[6] Auyeung B., Baron-Cohen S., Wheelwright S., Allison C. (2008). "The Autism Spectrum Quotient: Children's Version (AQ-Child)" (PDF). *J. Autism Dev. Disord.* **38**(7):1230–1240. doi: 10.1007/s10803-007-0504-z. PMID 18064550. Retrieved 21/10/2011.

[7] Baron-Cohen S., Hoekstra R.A., Knickmeyer R., Wheelwright S. (2006). "The Autism-Spectrum Quotient (AQ)—adolescent version" (PDF). *J. Autism Dev. Disord.* **36**(3): 343–350. doi:10.1007/s10803-006-0073-6.

Other Online Tests

The nice thing about online tests is that you can take this from the comfort of your own home.

Here is a list of other online tests, you may want to consider looking at:

Broad Autism Phenotype Test – According to the website "This questionnaire is designed to measure the mild autistic traits present in people who are not actually autistic but have a genetic predisposition to autism."

<u>Aspie Quiz</u> — A slight variation of the AQ Test; this will measure neurodiverse and neurotypical traits in adults.

<u>Mind in the Eyes Test</u> – This is a test that evaluates capacity to read facial expressions.

Telling someone that you think they may have Asperger's Syndrome

Firstly, I would like to say that it has been a difficult decision to sit down and write. "How do I tell some they may have Asperger's?" is a question that I get asked a lot on this site and it is always a difficult one to answer.

I usually try to avoid giving specific advice, because I don't know the individual involved. So rather than providing you with the 'correct' answer or the correct things to say, I will try and leave it open and cover the issue from several angles and then leave it open for debate. At the end of the day, I believe we all need to make informed decisions about this subject.

Before I go into this issue, I think it's important for us to look inside, about <u>why</u> it's important to tell the person they may have Asperger's. I have seen relationship situations where one partner uses the 'fact' that the other partner is on the spectrum to win arguments or just to be right and

I believe this is totally the wrong motivation.

In many cases the actual diagnosis or awareness of whether a person has Asperger's Syndrome can be liberating. Understanding why one behaves and thinks the way one does can give the person a lot of self-acceptance. With that knowledge, an individual can also seek out techniques and therapies that can support them to have a better quality of life. Now this is a good motivation to make someone aware.

But....... it really depends on the individual. Some people are really not open to feedback. They do not invite it and they are really not open to it if it comes unsolicited. So if your loved one is in this bracket you need to be super aware because in trying to help, you run the danger of pushing the person away in the process and this is really not what you want. In these cases it can often be better to let the person come to their own conclusions and journey of self-discovery. However, if the person is more open and seeks advice, it can be easier.

I have talked to Renee Salas about this issue and we both agree it is a loaded but important subject. Renee has an excellent <u>post</u> where she discusses this issue from the point of view a parent. She suggests a number of questions one should ask oneself before going into the issue. I quite like them so I thought I would add them here. Try asking yourself these questions as part of the decision process about whether to talk to the person or not:

- Do I think this person would want to know?

- Do I think this person should know because it's what **I** want? Or is it what he/she would want?

- Do I want to tell this person because I think it will make things easier for him/her? (E.g. are they lost and struggling in areas, confused at their inability to 'fit in' or succeed?)

- What is this person's current view of Autism? This is a biggy. Autism still has so much negative stigma attached. If the person is not privy to the Autism community that we are a part of (i.e. bloggers/FB'ers/Twitterers who are working to bring the positives and successes to the forefront from an autistic point of view) their reaction would probably be one of anger. Then possibly fear and denial.

• Am I looking at this person as an individual, taking into consideration: family, friends, social circles, job/career?

• Is he/she overly concerned with what others think? Is he/she the type of person who might feel shame and worry over being stigmatised as a 'person with a disability'?

If the answers to the above convince you that it would be right to talk to the person or make them aware, here are a few ways I can think of to playfully or gently make him/her aware of the symptoms of Asperger's Syndrome.

Watch movies on Asperger's Syndrome and Autism

Many times people in the general public are not aware of the symptoms and mannerisms of Asperger's. By watching movies and TV series that portray the character and personality of people with the condition, you can initially raise awareness. Often the person will recognise traits in the characters and it may be a way to very slowly raise awareness to the point where the subject can eventually be broached.

Here is a list of Autism and Aspergers related movies: http://www.aspergerstestsite.com/598/aspergers-movies

Make the taking of a test a playful activity

So, just like any game, often people like to partake as a bit of fun. Taking turns to take the Test for Aspergers can be a playful way to get someone to take an initial screening assessment. You can also send the link to someone and say something like "I got a score of x, am curious what you got". The important thing is that it has to be done playfully and you have to feel the person is open to receive the information. It should also not be done in a competitive way that comes across as "I am normal and you have something wrong with you."

The test is available on our website as well as a Google Android or IOS application.

Highlighting the genius

To many there is a big stigma with having Asperger's; it is deemed as something negative. But if you would intentionally mention the positive aspects of people who have Asperger's and suggest that your friend has similar traits, it may be a way to get that person to open up to the possibility.

Read this — it sounds like you

Well, this isn't my idea, but I found it on a forum. Some became aware of their nature by someone emailing them a link that said, "Read this, it sounds like you." Apparently, this casual suggestion left the person free to decide for themselves. It also didn't cause offense or bring up defenses because the person could see why it sounded like them. You could try a similar thing, giving them a link to a good introduction to an article about Asperger's such as: http://www.autism.org.uk/about-autism/autism-and-asperger-syndrome-an-introduction/what-is-asperger-syndrome.aspx.

Talking directly to the person

Talking directly to the person is all about the right approach.

The National Autistic Society recommend that you consider who is the right person to broach the subject. For example, the person may be more able to accept the results of the conversation if it comes from a friend or sibling rather than a parent. The NAS encourage one to carefully plan out what will be said in a way that is diplomatic. You can check out this article, which has a few good ideas on how to handle the issue: http://www.autism.org.uk/about-autism/autism-and-asperger-syndrome-an-introduction/what-is-asperger-syndrome/asperger-syndrome-broaching-the-subject.aspx.

So, as I said at the beginning, this is a very difficult and sensitive issue to talk about. You will need to adopt any of the ideas to the person, but remember they are only ideas. Talking to people and communicating difficult issues is a fine art. No one can truly teach you this art; it's something you need to develop inside of yourself. If you are not confident that what you say or do will be well received, perhaps you should not. In such cases, just respect the fact that the person will be open to face or acknowledge things in themselves when they are ready.

Adults with Asperger's – Getting a late diagnosis

By Cynthia Kim

More and more adults are being diagnosed with Autism Spectrum Disorder (ASD) in their thirties, forties and beyond. Not surprisingly, one of the most common ways that adults realise they are on the spectrum is in the wake of having a child diagnosed with ASD.

Some parents start out researching Autism as an explanation for their child's struggles and realise that an ASD diagnosis would explain a lot about their own life, too. The first clue for others is when a professional who works with their child mentions that Autism can run in families. Regardless of how it happens, there is often a sense of disbelief at that initial Aha! moment.

I remember the exact moment I first thought I might have Asperger's Syndrome. I was listening to an NPR story about David Finch, the author of "The Journal of Best Practices". Finch described an online quiz that his wife asked him to take because she recognised so many Aspie traits in him.

As he and his wife described the quiz questions, for the first time I realised that Asperger's Syndrome (AS) is more than just social awkwardness and that I'm more than just painfully shy. The symptoms that stood out most for me were the ones I'd never known were 'symptoms' of anything other than my personality: attachment to routine, resistance to change, special interests, a need to be alone. I found myself nodding along with the program, shocked at how much I had in common with Finch, and yet not quite believing I could have gone four decades without realizing something so critical about myself.

The first thing I did was search for a screening quiz like the one described in the radio program. I took the AQ and the Aspie Quiz, certain that one of them would prove me wrong, even as I repeatedly scored in the high range for AS traits on each.

I sat there at my desk for long minutes. Could it be possible that I'd been autistic all my life and not known it? I'd always known that I was different.

I'd been labelled 'shy', 'weird', 'introverted', 'geeky'. But what if I wasn't just weird? What if this thing called Asperger's Syndrome explained everything about me that was different?

That was an exciting thought. If it was true, it gave me a whole new way of thinking about my life. But the excitement soon wore off and I was faced with what to do with this realization. It turns out there aren't many resources for adults with ASD, especially those who aren't formally diagnosed.

Is a diagnosis necessary?

A diagnosis opens the door to services at school and home for children, but what about for adults? If you've made it into mid-life without a diagnosis, you may find yourself wondering if getting diagnosed really matters. I went back and forth for months on the question of whether to seek a professional diagnosis. Eventually I decided to pursue a diagnosis, primarily for peace of mind. I needed to know that I wasn't imagining everything.

There are many reasons you may choose to pursue a diagnosis as an adult: to access services, to request accommodations at work or school, or to increase the likelihood that therapy or counselling takes your ASD traits into account. Whatever your reason, it's important to be aware that the diagnostic process is more challenging for adults than for children.

Many adults run into difficulties with access. There are still few professionals qualified to diagnose adults. The process is often expensive and not covered by health insurance. Misdiagnosis is common. And some adults choose not to seek a formal diagnosis out of concern that it may lead to stigma or bias, or create practical limitations like not being able to join the military or having parental rights questioned.

The self-discovery process

Obviously, this is a decision that you'll want to give a lot of thought to. As you do, it can be helpful to spend time on self-discovery, testing out your suspicion that you're on the spectrum through research and introspection.

Self-discovery can include:

Learning more about ASD in adults: if you have a child with ASD, you're familiar with ASD traits. While the diagnostic criteria are the same for all ages, autism looks different in adults than it does in children. As we age, we develop a range of coping mechanisms that can mask typical symptoms, making them harder to identify. There can also be gender-related differences. Good sources of information about adult ASD include books like Tony Attwood's "The Complete Guide to Asperger's Syndrome" and blogs and vlogs by autistic adults.

Assessing ASD traits in yourself: based on your reading and research, make a list of traits you see in yourself. Talk with one or more trusted persons in your life about your self-assessment. Share a list of <u>ASD traits</u> (<u>female ASD traits</u>) with them. Do they see the same traits that you perceive? Do they see traits you haven't considered?

Looking back at childhood: if you have access to childhood records (baby book, report cards, etc.) or home movies, it can be helpful to look for typical early signs of ASD. If possible, you can also ask your parents or caregivers about specific behaviours. Often, an adult diagnosis will involve answering questions about your childhood, so any information you can gather before an assessment will be helpful.

By the time you've completed your research, you should have a good idea of whether ASD is a good fit for you. Many adults are content with this and choose to self-identify as Aspie or autistic based on their self-discovery process. Others feel the need–or have a specific reason—to seek out a professional diagnosis.

Seeking an adult ASD assessment

If you decide to pursue a professional diagnosis, it's important to find a psychologist, psychiatrist or neuropsychologist experienced in diagnosing adults with ASD. If your child has received a diagnosis, his or her clinician may be able to refer you to someone who does adult assessments. Other options for finding providers who do adult evaluations include: online resources like the Pathfinders for Autism website; recommendations from other autistic adults; parents of autistic children; teaching/research university hospitals; and local non-profit autism service organizations.

Whatever path you take to find someone who can evaluate you, know that it won't likely be a direct route. It's okay to feel like the biggest first step you can manage right now is to make a list of providers to contact. It may take weeks or months to start making those calls and yet more months to commit to meeting with a professional or scheduling an evaluation, especially if you are simultaneously dealing with the demands of being your autistic child's advocate.

Ultimately, most adults find that an autism diagnosis is a positive thing. It provides an explanation for why we've always felt different and is the first step in assembling a toolbox filled with new coping skills and adaptations.

Why Asperger's Hasn't Existed since May 2013

Yes the title sounds odd. Having talked previously about getting an official diagnosis, we are now saying it has gone away. However things are not quite that simple. It simply got reclassified into something else (at least for official purposes).

Let me explain: DSM version 5 (DSM-V) was modified to remove the diagnosis of Asperger's and reclassify those showing those symptoms under the general Autism Spectrum umbrella. The DSM is the d facto tool most doctors use to diagnose individuals, based on their characteristics. The decision to move Asperger's was based on their belief that it would better serve people on the Autism Spectrum.

The problem with this move is that there are people who had been previously diagnosed with Asperger's under DSM-IV but could no longer qualify for a diagnosis under the Autism Spectrum umbrella. This caused a lot of anger for many people in the Asperger's community. They felt the move would make them unrepresented and that they'd simply be absorbed wholesale into the new classification.

There is growing evidence that Asperger's is different to Autism in terms of brain connectivity. In response to the DSM reclassification, there was a research study carried out by Frank Duffy, M.D. He used electroencephalography (EEG) recordings to measure the amount of signalling occurring between brain areas. His findings were that "The ASP population appears to constitute a neurophysiologically identifiable, normally distributed entity within the higher functioning tail of the ASD population distribution." You can read more details about the study at: http://www.biomedcentral.com/1741-7015/11/175.

Alongside these differences, there are also other differences, such as developmental delays that only become apparent in children with Asperger's as they get older. They typically do not experience the same language delays as children with other elements of Autism Spectrum Disorders.

Some estimates suggest that one third of people who would have previously qualified for a diagnosis of either Autism or Asperger's will no longer fit into either diagnosis category as a result of reclassification. This then has implications for the level of support and insurance-based services that would have previously been available to that individual.

Personally, I find the reclassification trend disturbing. However, the good news is that the European diagnostic classification (the ICD framework) does continue to recognise Asperger's as a separate subgroup.

My hope is that as awareness of the issue is raised, the reclassification will be reversed in the next version of the DSM.

PDD-NOS

In this book, we thought we should include PDD-NOS as this is a slightly alternative diagnosis given to Asperger's in the DSM-IV.

PDD-NOS, or Pervasive Developmental Disorder Not Otherwise Specified, is a type of diagnosis given to individuals on the Autism Spectrum. As a diagnosis, it fits somewhere between Asperger's Syndrome and classic Autism.

Often it is used as a kind of catch all for those that do not fully fit into either category. It can be used as a diagnosis when there is little or no data to support a typical Autism diagnosis with regard to the early part of one's life. Usually classic Autism features developmental issues and social retardation from an early age. With PDD-NOS this information is not always necessary for medical professionals to make an attempt at diagnosis.

The symptoms of PDD-NOS

While PDD-NOS has many of the same characteristics, the major symptoms used to diagnose are:

- •   social impairments

- •   communication impairments

- •   repetitive behaviours.

While these are not the only symptoms, there are other behaviours associated with other conditions that are common with PDD. These include: Autistic Disorder, Asperger's Syndrome, Rett Syndrome and Childhood Disintegrative Disorder.

DSM Criteria

DSM, commonly known as the Diagnostic and Statistical Manual of Mental Disorders, is widely recognised around the world by various psychiatric associations as the standard for clinical diagnosis.

We have included the DSM-IV criteria rather than the later DSM-V one as it (DSM-V) subsequently grouped Asperger's Syndrome together with the more general Autism Spectrum Disorder category and I feel that PDD-NOS still deserves a mention in the old category.

The <u>DSM-IV definition</u> of the category for Pervasive Developmental Disorders Not Otherwise Specified is:

"This category should be used when there is a severe and pervasive impairment in the development of reciprocal social interaction or verbal and nonverbal communication skills, or when stereotyped behavior, interests, and activities are present, but the criteria are not met for a specific pervasive developmental disorder, schizophrenia, schizotypal personality disorder, or avoidant personality disorder. For example, this category includes "atypical autism" – presentations that do not meet the criteria for autistic disorder because of late age of onset, atypical symptomatology, or subthreshold symptomatology, or all of these."

The methodology behind PDD-NOS diagnosis is now becoming a very contentious issue. Many argue that the definition is too weak and that even medical professionals disagree about the correct diagnosis. This could well be a classic example of being placed in a box.

Testing for PDD-NOS

Unlike with Asperger's, there unfortunately does not exist a wide range of testing materials for self-diagnosis. The condition, by its very nature, is difficult to diagnose, as it is, in essence, an umbrella for many conditions within the Autism Spectrum. If you are looking for clues as to the likelihood of having Pervasive Developmental Disorder, we can recommend either using the generic autism quotient test or this experimental assessment on the childbrain website.

If you are concerned whether you may have the condition, we strongly recommend that you visit a medical professional to get more professional advice.

Where is PDD-NOS in DSM-V?

With the advent of DSM-V things became a lot less diverse in all areas of the Autism Spectrum. Classic autism, Asperger's and PDD-NOS have been rolled into a single Autism Spectrum category.

This is a cause of controversy for many members of the autistic community, who feel that the change in diagnostic criteria is unwelcome.

Generic diagnosis such as this never truly represents the true condition of the individual. Some boxes may be ticked but not others, but for the medical professional it does seem easier to give someone a more generic label than to take the time and really understand what is going on.

PDD-NOS resources

There is a neat checklist that can be used for spotting diagnosis on the National Autism Resources website.

Also check out Barbara Quinns book on Pervasive Developmental Disorder, which we highly recommend as a resource guide on the subject.

You can also find a list of recommended books and other resources on our website.

Comorbid Conditions

Comorbid conditions are a set of additional conditions that can occur alongside the primary condition.

In layman's terms this means that people with AS often have other conditions. These may include:

- anxiety disorders

- ADHD

- bipolar Disorder

- bowel disease

- dyspraxia

- dyslexia

- OCD

- Tourette's Syndrome

- sleep disorders.

For anyone reading the list above, don't necessarily be disturbed. Just because you may qualify for an Asperger's diagnosis, it does not mean you have all of these conditions. It's just possible that you have some of them.

Dealing with the diagnosis

Everybody is different when it comes to responding to the diagnosis that they have Asperger's or Autism.

For some, it is a relief because it helps you understand why you are the way you are. You have a reference point and you can understand that there are many people around the world with the same condition.

But for many people, accepting the diagnosis is not easy; it can bring memories from the past about occasions when the symptoms were most present. Perhaps from social events, childhood or school.

It's easy to think of ourselves as different and inferior. We don't feel good enough and we often suffer from low self-esteem.

One of the most important things to remember during the period following diagnosis is that Asperger's can be a gift as well as a curse. Yes it's true, sometimes we struggle with life and social skills that are easy for many neurotypical (NT) individuals. However, people with Asperger's

Syndrome have many different abilities and qualities. The ability to see and understand the world in different ways with a different perception can add so many gifts to the world.

If you haven't seen the <u>movie</u> about Temple Grandin's struggle with Autism and her subsequent achievements in life, we recommend you do. Not only did Temple find a way to overcome the emotional distress, but she also gained a Ph.D. in animal science and became an internationally recognised speaker in the autistic community. Temple is truly an example to us all.

Without the qualities of Asperger's Syndrome, we wouldn't have the pioneering theory of relativity that was developed by Albert Einstein, or the widespread adoption of the Windows operating system when Bill Gates created Microsoft. It's important to find your contribution to the world, however big or small.

Chapter 3 — Aspects of Asperger's Syndrome

Asperger's and thinking differently

I just wanted to share this video with you today; it kind of sums up why there is nothing wrong with thinking differently: https://www.youtube.com/watch?v=e5LH78Vy5Ck.

Even though this advertisement was commissioned by Apple, it's very interesting to note that in this video there are quite a few characters who are speculated to have had Asperger's Syndrome, including: Albert Einstein, Thomas Edison, Alfred Hitchcock, Jim Henson, Amelia Earhart and Pablo Picasso (see more on famous people with AS below).

One of the symptoms associated with Asperger's

Syndrome is the narrow range of interests that one can become obsessive with. Often people with Autism develop 'special hobbies', becoming totally obsessive around a certain interest at the expense of all others. The capability to block out all distractions and become highly focused has led to some amazing advancements in technology and scientific understanding. Often the capacity to recognise patterns that others do not, as well as the long hours devoted to the pursuit of one's passion, has helped those on the Autistic Spectrum become recognised as geniuses.

Albert Einstein and Thomas Edison are two of the more famous individuals that are believed to have had Autism. These two are responsible for the Theory of Relativity and the electric light bulb, respectively.

It is interesting that world-renowned Autism speaker Temple Grandin once referred to NASA as a sheltered workshop for people on the Autistic Spectrum. Her opinion is that people with Autism are true innovators, and she was once quoted as saying, "If the world was left to you socialites, nothing would get done and we would still be in caves talking to each other."

Famous people with Autism and Asperger's

So as the number of individuals with autism and Asperger's continues to increase and they become a greater part of the public conversation regarding research and treatment, one question that comes up frequently is "What famous people have Autism?".

Well, to most of those familiar with this disorder, the idea of someone famous with Asperger's would almost be considered an oxymoron as the word 'famous' usually conjures up images of someone who is always in the spotlight and likes going to social engagements or just hanging out with their friends. For those with Autism, however, nothing could be further from the truth.

One contributing factor to this is that unfortunately for many of those who have, or might have, Autism, it is something that can easily be misunderstood and for doctors it can also be misdiagnosed. In some situations, it can go undetected as late as into adulthood and for even a few, it may only come through their own perseverance to understand themselves. So why is that?

For starters, unlike many others who have autism, people with Asperger's rarely display a delay in either language or cognitive development. So while they may have a lack of social skills, their ability to communicate can still help them get through their day-to-day routine.

In addition to that, if Asperger's is difficult to diagnose for doctors, then it might stand to reason that this would also be true for the public. For those in the limelight, like those in television, radio or the movies, for example, perception is something that is important to them and thus something they strive to control when they appear in the public eye.

Putting that aside, though, if we're able to remove the cameras, makeup and the like, who are some of the famous contemporary people who have Autism? One footnote to add here is that, for many of these people, their diagnosis is based on self-evidence and is in fact not medically proven.

With that said, this group includes:

Paul Allen (entrepreneur)

Dan Aykroyd (actor)

Bob Dylan (musician)

Bill Gates (entrepreneur)

Temple Grandin (author)

Al Gore (politician)

Daryl Hannah (actress)

Alfred Hitchcock (director)

Garrison Keillor (public radio)

Clay Marzo (surfer)

Craig Nicholls (musician)

Keith Olberman (sportscaster)

Tim Page (author)

Oliver Sacks (author)

Charles Schultz (cartoonist)

James Taylor (musician)

Andy Warhol (artist)

Robin Williams (comedian — deceased).

In addition, there are many historical people that are thought to have had Asperger's and they include:

Jane Austen (writer)

Ludwig Van Beethoven (musician)

Thomas Edison (inventor)

Albert Einstein (scientist)

Henry Ford (automobile maker)

Benjamin Franklin (politician)

Abraham Lincoln (politician)

Henry Thoreau (writer/philosopher)

Mark Twain (writer).

In many ways we may never truly know how many other famous people may have Asperger's because, as mentioned previously, those under the spotlight tend to prefer to control what the public does or doesn't see in regards to themselves. That said, what are some of the traits that these people exhibit that lead to that conclusion?

Some of these individuals, like Albert Einstein, are said to have had language delays as a child. Others, such as Bill Gates, were unable to develop peer relationships and still some, like Benjamin Franklin, had an obsession or even compulsion with order. All of these are examples of characteristics common to those with Autism.

Despite the challenges that Autism (and even Asperger's) presents, though, some of these people show, or have shown us, that one can overcome these obstacles and lead a happy and rewarding life. In fact, we see that by simply combining some of their unique traits, such as their ability to focus or strong perseverance along with their strong academics, they have shown that Autism can be a blessing whereas many may see it as a weakness.

Sensory processing issues

Sensory processing issues occur because signals in the brain don't get appropriately processed. There are several senses that can be affected:

- sound

- sight

- touch

- smell.

One's sensitivity levels very often drive behaviour and coping mechanisms, with hyposensitive people more likely to seek out stimulation of the senses as a soothing mechanism while hypersensitive people are likely to move away from things like loud noises etc.

Sensory processing issues are often major symptoms of Autism Spectrum Disorders. Sensory overload in many cases can end up being a trigger for other aspects of behaviour that people are familiar with, such as stimming and meltdowns.

The effects of overstimulation can be seen in these

moments, when certain sounds make a situation unbearable and high-level emotion and energy build up in the body until such a time as the person becomes overwhelmed and either begins stimming or having a meltdown.

Personally I can experience such moments when I hear a baby crying or someone drilling a hole in a wall. I can handle it for a few minutes but over time it eventually feels like the sound is going through me.

Equally it's also possible for one to be under sensitive and seek out stimulation from touch, sound or food as a way of self-soothing. This was actually one of the drivers for Temple Grandin making the squeeze machine in order to give her some sensory stimulation. The squeeze machine was for her a "magical device that would provide intense, pleasant pressure". She discovered the device while at her Aunt's ranch when observing a machine that squeezed cattle to relax them by placing wooden boards over the cattle's backs and sides. Temple decided to make a similar device for herself, which applied subtle pressure to her body when she pulled a cord. It replicates the body's natural healing feeling, which occurs when one receives a hug. Many people on the Autism Spectrum will know that while a hug from a human can be nourishing, the sensory stimulation that occurs as a result can also be overwhelming.

Sensory Processing Disorder

A look at Asperger's Syndrome and anxiety

According to conservative estimates, 65% of adults with Asperger's Syndrome suffer from anxiety and depression compared to 18% of the general population.

Everyone experiences the effects of anxiety slightly differently. It can come in many forms, including:

Panic Disorder

People suffering from panic disorder can experience sudden and repeated attacks of fear.

The person senses that impending disaster is close by and that they will lose control of the situation. It can result in shortness of breath, heart palpitations, chest pain, hot flushes and/or light headedness.

Social Phobia

Social Phobia is a fear of being judged by others. It often represents itself by excessive self-consciousness and anxiety in everyday situations. It's also possible that it triggers off panic attacks that are associated with Panic Disorder. Often this fear makes us withdraw from society, being afraid to go out.

Generalised Anxiety Disorder (GAD)

GAD represents itself in the form of worrying excessively or irrationally. It may be combined with symptoms such as headaches or insomnia.

Obsessive Compulsive Disorder (OCD)

This form of anxiety is expressed in the need to check things repeatedly and unnecessarily, such as repeatedly checking the door is locked or that one has washed their hands.

A look at Aspergers and Anxiety

Often the presence of anxiety in people with Asperger's is overlooked because one's internal state or mental setting is hard to communicate and explain to non-autists. But living with anxiety can affect body image, motivation, behaviour, and even the ability to think correctly.

From doing several workshops in personal

growth, I have had insights that anxiety often comes to the surface when there are other emotions that want to come to the surface. It feels like the anxiety is a distraction from the other feelings. For example, I feel sad and can't allow myself to cry. I become anxious because I don't want to allow that feeling. The same if I'm afraid or angry. Sometimes there is an apprehension about what could happen. I determine the future will be similar to the past and therefore become anxious about a perceived negative outcome for a future event. But pretty much always, if I go deeper into the experience, it is pretty much always an emotion that wants to come to the surface.

A common approach many people take in response to anxiety is to isolate themselves as a response to the outside world.

While many search for a 'cure all' pill, it is important that this issue is dealt with in more ways than at a purely pharmaceutical level. While medication makes up a significant part of a successful treatment plan, the mindset itself has to be remedied before lasting improvement can be noted. Do not just see medication as an easy way out; it is merely a tool to assist you in self-improvement.

Autism-related anxiety is typically characterised by depression, overwhelming discomfort around people, heart palpitations, profuse sweating, mutism or pressured speech, obsessive and repetitive thoughts, and an overwhelming desire to escape the current surroundings. Firstly paying attention to, and becoming aware of, these symptoms already leads to a noticeable improvement. If it is appropriate to the given situation, listening to downtempo (chill) music greatly alleviates anxiety.

If you are experiencing intrusive thoughts, imagine them floating away beyond the top of your head. After a while, they will slow down or cease. Try to inhale slowly through your nose, and exhale slowly through your mouth. In severe cases of anxiety: breathe in, hold for 8–10 seconds, breathe out. Repeat this until you feel better. Eventually your body and your unconscious mind will get used to doing this and automatically adapt your breathing pattern.

If you are looking for more techniques for dealing

with day-to-day anxiety, I cover the issue in more depth in my book "Emotional Mastery for Adults with Asperger's".

The relationship between Asperger's and depression

Sadly, depression is part of life for those living with Asperger's Syndrome. Yet it appears to be an often-ignored part of the condition.

According to research carried out at the University of Gothenburg, up to 70% of young Adults with Asperger's Syndrome suffer from depression. This is in stark contrast to the 18% depression rate in the general population.

Even though individuals with Autism are more likely to become depressed, they are less likely to pursue treatment because they may rather internalise the pain they are feeling than seek outside assistance. It's also possible that they may be unable to articulate what exactly it is they are feeling. Difficulty in reading the facial expressions and body language of people who are on the Autistic Spectrum also means that depression is not easily observable from the outside.

The relationship between Aspergers and depression

Whether the depression is a result of social stigmatisation, low self-worth or other causes, the end result is the same: a deep feeling of isolation, loss of motivation, immense sadness, and deeply impaired quality of life. In addition to the regular symptoms of depression, people with Autism may experience a worsening of communication skills, repetitive movements, compulsions, isolation and changes in time perception.

There are two main causes of depression. The first is where past traumas and emotional buildup cause one to get depressed. The other is a chemical imbalance in the brain. It is not uncommon for the first cause (if left untreated) to develop into the second.

While the chemical imbalance seems to be an easy explanation in the majority of cases, it is often not directly the case with adults with Asperger's. Living with Autism and Asperger's, there is often a daily struggle that takes place involving obsessive behaviour, alienation and coordination problems. An inability to communicate or express the feelings that get raised from these circumstances often brings on the onset of depression. When one thinks about the word itself — depression — it is actually the opposite of expression.

Regardless of the exact causes, the fact remains that this problem clearly exists and needs to be dealt with on a larger scale than has been previously done by the medical and social professions.

Two of the most effective ways to combat both anxiety and depression are exercise and meditation. These flagship treatments are talked about so often that one may believe that they are simply hearsay from people who do not know what they are talking about. Especially in a depressive state, this may seem like a reasonable and acceptable explanation. It is not. This is absolutely not the case. The most common causes of depression in any individual are lack of exercise and the inability to control intrusive thoughts, which are both effectively remedied by exercise and meditation.

Because both exercise and meditation release helpful neurotransmitters and jumpstart the brain's regenerative capabilities, they should absolutely be the core of any treatment plan.

Too many people do not deal with depression until it actually occurs, but where is the harm in trying to prevent it? Staying active and mindful is a great asset to anyone, depressed or not.

Especially in Autism, it is crucial to be wary of depression, since it quickly becomes progressively harder to treat.

If regular exercise and meditation are not enough, one could try to search for a fulfilling hobby that can provide immersion to stop becoming engrossed in obsessive thoughts. This would provide a healthy distraction and possibly a way out of the initial stages of depression. Staying preoccupied is a coping strategy that works for a lot of people, but this highly depends on the individual.

Another common issue is diet. Many Autistic people have an aversion to certain foods due to texture, colour and taste. This hypersensitivity to certain sensory aspects of food leads the individual to avoid them. What is often not taken into consideration is that this can result in numerous nutritional deficiencies that significantly worsen depression. A lack of zinc, vitamin B6, B12, or D in the daily diet is an extremely common cause of depression.

It is important to notice the signs and symptoms of depression at their onset, and catch them while they are easily malleable and not yet internalised. This is necessary because the symptoms of Autism, such as obsessive ruminations, can solidify a negative mindset and make it difficult to escape. One could argue that Autism does not predispose to depression itself, but rather to preserving it once even a small episode occurs. The key here would be to focus more on reframing one's own perspectives with the intent of prevention, rather than waiting to deal with something until it becomes too much of a burden. Therefore, individuals with Autism should realise the urgency of the need for treatment, whether through therapy, medication, or a combination of both.

Asperger's and OCD – Obsessional Behaviours, Diagnosis and Treatment Options

Copyright 2012 by Carol Edwards

CBT Dip.HE (D) Dip.OCD (D) ASD credits – CRB checked

Carol is a Cognitive Behavioural Therapist who specialises in the area of OCD. She became interested in the area after one of her family members became misdiagnosed with Asperger's Syndrome, when in fact they actually had OCD. This article illustrates that while the two conditions may overlap, they are not always the same.

Asperger's Syndrome

Asperger's Syndrome, often referred to as Asperger's or AS, comes under the umbrella of Autistic Spectrum Disorders; it is a complex developmental disability that affects the way a person communicates and relates to the people around them. The term 'Autistic Spectrum' is often used because the condition varies from person to person. For example, some individuals who have accompanying learning disabilities are usually placed at the less able end of the spectrum, while others who have average, or above, intelligence are placed at the more able end of the spectrum (Asperger's).

Despite the various differences, everyone with the disorder has difficulty with what is known as the 'triad of impairments'. These are:

- social interaction and social skills

- social communication

- social imagination.

Obsessive Compulsive Disorder

Obsessive Compulsive Disorder, or OCD, is characterised by intrusive thoughts, ideas and images which often follow compulsive behaviours. These can be overt and also covert. For example, an individual whose OCD variation revolves around contamination fears may openly display an urge to repeatedly wash his/her hands (overt), whereas a person who suffers from disturbing thoughts and images may try to cancel these intrusions out by using a counter phrase or praying ritual in his mind (covert). Both behaviours serve to reduce the anxiety brought on by these intrusions, but only momentarily.

Unless there is an autistic overlap or other pervasive developmental disorder, a person with OCD usually does not present with problems associated with the triad of impairments.

Social imagination

In this article, we'll be looking at the triad to distinguish what the driving force behind obsessional behaviours means and if the findings suggest whether a person has developed social imagination or not. Observing how a person reacts in response to his/her compulsions or rituals can provide us with clues; therefore, let's consider two individuals with obsessive behaviours:

Jack has an obsessive compulsion where he feels compelled to line up food items in order of size in the kitchen cupboard while Jill repeats a ritual which involves lining up a collection of ornaments in a cabinet in the family's lounge.

While Jack is generally an honest person, he has none-the-less learned to use deception to manage his OCD. In other words when he is prevented from doing a ritual he uses his imagination to find ways to figure out how to complete the act. For instance, while watching TV, Jack's wife often prevents him from repeatedly checking that there isn't a tin, bottle or packet out of place in the kitchen cupboard. This increases Jack's anxiety but he wants to avoid conflict; therefore, he uses every trick up his sleeve so that he can fulfil his compelling need to check. Using deception provides him with the opportunity to relieve himself of anxiety, e.g. making up the excuse that he's 'just nipping through to the kitchen for a snack'.

Now let's consider Jill's obsessional behaviour. Basically, the imagination is in the act itself, which is part of her daily routine. When Jill lines up the ornaments she experiences organised satisfaction, rather than anxiety relief. When Jill's mother tries to stop her, explaining that they have to leave for Jill's scheduled appointment, Jill feels extreme annoyance to the point of anger, just like any person might if they were, for example, prevented from finishing their housework or something else and in the order they do it. The confused interaction between mother and daughter causes such distress that the appointment has to be cancelled.

What does this mean?

First, Jack can work around his compulsion because he understands that his thoughts affect his feelings and thus behaviours. The **thought** is "A bottle is out of place in the kitchen cupboard", which follows with the **feeling,** "When I'm prevented from checking, my anxiety rises", which leads to **deceptive behaviour**, e.g."I'll pretend I need a snack". To add to this, Jack is not only able to understand the connection between his own thoughts, feelings and behaviours, he is also capable of grasping the thoughts, feelings and behaviours of others, hence the deception towards his wife. This tells us that he has developed social understanding which fits neatly with the 'theory of mind' (Baron-Cohen *et al.* 1985*). What's sad, however, is that while Jack goes to ridiculous lengths to perform his compulsions, he knows the behaviours are attributed to OCD, not him, and he wants to stop.

Second, we've already established that Jill's daily routine involves lining up the ornaments in the family cabinet. Her behaviour when prevented from doing this reveals that social imagination might be lacking, e.g. faking illness to avoid going out so that she can stay home and finish her ritual. Further, the difficult interaction with her mother and her inability to grasp that failing to turn up for an appointment can be problematic for others involved indicates that her obsessional behaviour is stereotyped and therefore characteristic of Asperger's Syndrome. Jill fights her own corner honestly and has no conscious thoughts about whom and what the obsessional ritual is attributed to, and she doesn't want to stop. So does this imply a lack of social imagination, meaning Jill has not developed a theory of mind? Possibly, but not necessarily as it could be that this area of functioning requires intervention to help tease it into consciousness, thus improving social awareness and world perception.

*Theory of mind

Baron-Cohen speculates that having a theory of mind is what gives us the unique (to humans) ability to work together and execute complex interactions. In other words we are able to understand that we and others have minds with knowledge, feelings, beliefs, motivations, intentions, and so on, which includes presuming our own and others' mental states and then being able to explain and predict the behaviours arising from this. Humans are able to assess that others may hold false beliefs about themselves and the world around them. Baron-Cohen's research suggests that individuals on the Autistic Spectrum lack a theory of mind and therefore do not have the mental capacity to imagine the world from the perspective of others, which includes failing to question beliefs about themselves or others. They apparently live in a state of certainty in terms of what others may think about them; that is, what someone says is what they mean, and so on. You can find more information on this topic at: www.social-science.co.uk/corestudies/ titled *"Does the autistic child have a theory of mind?"*

Treatment for OCD

Some say anxiety is the source of OCD, which suggests a neurobiological condition to which pharmacological treatment in the form of Selective Serotonin Reuptake Inhibitors (SSRIs) is the primary tool. Others suggest it's the other way around, in which case a psychological approach to the problem is favoured. The psychological model is viewed from a social learning perspective, is specific in its approach with its cognitive and behavioural strategies and involves exposure response prevention (real or imagined). Its aim is to target obsessions, compulsions and doubt resulting from three underlying factors that maintain OCD: 1) fear 2) anxiety and 3) threat. Depression may also be a factor, which is often secondary to OCD, a result of the disruption caused in a person's life. There is some evidence which suggests the cognitive approach is as effective as the medical approach (SSRIs) in terms of this treatment modifying biological parameters (*Understanding Obsessive-Compulsive and Related Disorders*: www.ocd.stanford.edu). However, the level of OCD severity and secondary depression is not overlooked here, in which case medication combined with a biobehavioural approach is often an option.

A cognitive dilemma for those with

Asperger's

The cognitive approach casts doubt for those on the high end of the Autistic Spectrum, which is, since this type of therapy challenges the individual's belief system and focuses on bringing awareness of the psychological features of OCD, how does this fair when it comes to treating individuals with the disorder if they also have Asperger's? With regards to Baron-Cohen's theory and this being correct and in terms of those with AS sharing some features of autism, there is, however, no delay in language and cognitive development; so the answer in most cases has to be that the prognosis is good.

Back to choosing the right treatment options for OCD

The right choice of treatment takes into account many more factors than already discussed, such as whether pharmacotherapy should be considered; for instance, if a client refuses psychological treatment or has poor response to behavioural methods. Likewise, behaviour therapy might be the appropriate choice if the client refuses medication or if drug therapy is ineffective, if the client is pregnant, is a child etc. Further, a combined approach might be considered a better option because it offers the best of both treatments, especially if the client's condition has become entrenched over a number of years and/or if the person has depression or other overlapping conditions, or another distinguished disorder such as Asperger's or Bipolar. In extreme cases, hospitalisation may have to be discussed as a treatment option, such as when a client's condition is so debilitating that her contamination fears, for example, are so severe that she isolates herself from other people, including family members; in which case her overall health (and her family's well-being) is clearly at risk.

What happens when the wrong diagnosis is given?

A true diagnosis for both Asperger's and OCD can often be confusing. I have known children and adults diagnosed with AS whose traits include aversions to foods touching each other, social avoidance, touch issues, and so on, only to find these features were associated with contamination fears and other OCD problems. I have also come across people diagnosed with OCD appearing to present with contamination fears associated with food who have later revealed that they preferred their food placed on their plate in a particular order, not because they feared getting germs from food items touching each other. Some individuals also found social interaction difficult because they were touch-sensitive, not germ-obsessed, which is more likely to be characteristic of Asperger's, not OCD. These examples only touch the surface but the bigger picture suggests there might be some ambiguity regarding certain statements/questions when determining diagnosis. Thus it is crucial that the person is clear about what box he is actually ticking during assessment for either (or both) diagnosis. Further, during an assessment, be sure about what questions are being asked and what they mean before answering.

How to tell the difference between an OCD and an Asperger's behaviour

To help differentiate an OCD obsession from one relating to AS is to recognise that an OCD episode usually follows three stages: a) a trigger situation b) the obsessive thought content immediately after the trigger situation and c) the compulsive behaviour that follows to reduce anxiety. In contrast, an Asperger's obsession could be a preoccupation with detail. Consider the true example in the following scenario:

George is in a pub with his colleagues, John and Sarah. John puts his glass on the table, but the glass is an inch out of line with Sarah's. George is very aware of this and he is finding it difficult to engage in social interaction. This is an OCD **trigger situation** but his distraction could easily be confused with having a lack of social skills, indicating an Asperger's trait. The **thought content** that follows George's trigger situation is that his mother will die (magical thinking) if he doesn't align John's glass with Sarah's. His anxiety rises but he doesn't want to appear ridiculous so he distracts John and Sarah by standing up and deliberately tipping his own drink over (thankfully there was only a mouthful left), at which moment he surreptitiously brings Sarah's glass forward to match John's **(compulsive behaviour)**. What makes things socially worse for George is that he is equally concerned with the mole (or shall we say beauty spot!) on Sarah's upper lip — this type of obsessive focus during interaction suggests a symptom of Asperger's, especially because the beauty spot didn't fit quite centre with the philtrum (middle of the upper lip and below the nose), which could have triggered a further OCD episode in terms of alignment or symmetry obsession, but it didn't because the attention was on detail; that is, the beauty spot itself, nothing else. Here there are two separate conditions going on at the same time but what is interesting is that George's OCD incident highlights that a theory of mind is intact (social imagination); however, this is (or appears to be) absent during the 'beauty spot' situation. If we gauge George's OCD at 75% and his Asperger's at 25% then this becomes clear in terms of a muddled social imagination. Imagine, however, if the percentage is turned the other way around. Now predict what it must be like for someone coping socially with 100% criteria for Asperger's. The point here is that each person's situation is unique for which they deserve a unique intervention plan to decipher their confusion and help them cope better in what must be, at times, a socially incomprehensible world. The earlier treatment is applied the better, because behavioural traits can become fixed over the years, which means intervention might prove more challenging, not only for the individual but also for the practitioners involved.

My Thoughts

As a qualified CBT therapist, specialising in OCD and Asperger's, my aim is to separate each set of symptoms from the other in terms of providing a suitable intervention plan for the individual. I have seen social perception problems in those with and without AS and therefore keep an open mind about Baron-Cohen's theory, since each person is unique. Therefore using complementary therapy in the form of
cognitive behavioural therapy to help change faulty perceptions to conquer OCD for those with or without Asperger's (which would include additional management of behaviours associated with AS, e.g. social interaction) would be better than no treatment at all. My belief is that CBT (which may or may not include pharmacological intervention) continues for the present to be a favoured option for those with or without a formal diagnosis.

What Would Einstein Say About Autism Today?

Albert Einstein was one of the greatest and best-known scientists of his time. If he were alive today, what would he say about Autism? I believe it would go something like this:

You don't know how long I've been waiting to say these words to those affected by Autism. There are no words I can even conceive of to express my deepest concerns to those who are challenged with Autism. For some people it has been a tragedy, yet for others it is considered a gift. But for all of humanity it is time we came to understand Autism from the relativity of time.

To help me explain this I needed someone who would explore my Theory of Relativity and make their own great discoveries. I knew it would have to be someone like me, on the Autism Spectrum. Actually, when you think about it, many of us are on the spectrum, be it even on the most miniscule level, because very few people's minds perform at optimal perfection. Once you understand Autism from a new perspective you will appreciate your own differences for what they really are.

Furthermore, and most importantly, we get to respect each and every other person's differences in a whole new way. So from here I have to leave it up to my brilliant friends **Bushy Van Eck**, Author of "Prisoners of Our Minds", member of Mensa, with an IQ higher than most college professors, and his friend Clayton Nuckelt to help us understand Autism from the relativity of time.

A Short Story: Part Fiction, Part Science, Part Philosophy, All Heart

Written By Cornelius (Bushy) Van Eck and Clayton Nuckelt

By understanding Autism from the relativity of time, you will understand how it can be a tragedy for some people as well as a gift to others.

I have been ridiculed most of my life for being different. I have felt both gifted and tormented at the same time. I became obsessed searching for the answer as to why my mind works so differently than others'. My research is based on scientific data as well as my own observations and conclusions. For me, my dream has come true, getting the answers I was looking for. Please don't worry if you do not understand everything you are about to read, for it took me over 25 years to make this discovery.

Have you ever noticed it seems like the oddballs of the world help move us forward the most? For some people one profound moment of clarity opens them up to a whole new world of knowledge and takes them to a higher level of existence. I believe we are truly on the brink of this new expansion. It happened for me and I know it can happen for you too if you give it a chance. When I set out to discover the truth behind our existence, so many years ago, I certainly ended up getting more than I bargained for. I truly hope I can help you have one of those 'Moments of Clarity' and it brings new meaning to your life and those around you in a whole new way. When someone is interested in something they tend to want to learn more. Every person who opens their heart and mind can learn something that will have a deep impact in your own life. You can gain a new respect for autistic people now, having *infinite empathy* because you understand how it can be a tragedy for some people as well as a gift to others. We will now be able to respect each other's experiences, struggles and opinions, no longer offending one another.

The foundation to understanding Autism in a meaningful way

Because my intention is to make this simple and easy to understand, I am not going to clutter your mind with a lot of big scientific definitions but will include links for clarification. Once you gain a basic understanding of this theory, it may become an instant realisation that was always right in front of you but never explained in a meaningful way.

Just like we all have our own personal finger print, the same goes for our minds. To help us understand Autism and how it relates to time we need to understand what a unit of time is and what a moment of awareness entails. For most of us we know what a minute of time feels like. But why does time seem to go by faster as we age and slower when we are younger? How do our minds use up more time? And the most important question is: How can time perception problems help explain Autism symptoms?

The Theory of Time Perception, by

Cornelius (Bushy) Van Eck

Think of time as a sequencing of units. These units are called Planck units in Physics.

Each Planck unit is equal to 1 bit of data (or information or knowledge); these bits of data form sounds, words, colours, thoughts, touch, etc. into moments of awareness. In other words it takes so many required units of time, depending on the substance, to form a moment of awareness. Read the following paragraph over and over until it sinks in deep into your psyche, the human soul, mind, or spirit.

A moment of conscious awareness: the 'Miracle of life'

The more sophisticated and technological society gets, the more time we are using. Each *moment of awareness* consists of past, present and future Planck units of time. Play almost any video game today for what seems like a few minutes and ask yourself hours later "Where did the time go?" As we get older we obtain great amounts of data and become more intelligent. Each *moment of awareness* now requires many more Planck units of time. Example: in a flash of a second, when you see a picture of a steak dinner on the menu, you know everything about it from past, present and future. Past — *what it tastes like* (assuming you've had it before); present — *how much it costs*; future — *how much you will enjoy it*!

This *moment of awareness* took many units of time to process. The higher the data per *moment of awareness*, the more time will be perceived to have gone by. The lower the data per *moment of awareness*, the less time will be perceived to have gone by. If we truly want to live longer lives, then we must consider limiting technology that steals away our time. You now have a whole new meaning to 'Managing Your Time'.

Sensory Processing Disorder (SPD)

<u>Enhanced Motion Perception in Autism May Point to an Underlying Cause of the Disorder.</u> Now back to understanding Autism in a meaningful way so that you will be able to make sense of most new related research. How can an autistic person "see faster"? All of the data, or units of time and information, is first processed in the subconscious mind and for an average person the processing speed of data is very similar to that of other average people in performance. But what

happens when the data is being passed on to the conscious mind too fast or too slow, or too much or too little is attempting to be sent at once (for example, you are receiving too many sound bites of data)? It will create havoc for a person's sense of sound, hearing all the voices in a room all at once. The same would go for any perception of touch, sight, thought or similar. Once you get to conceptualise my theory, you will be able to apply it to many mental differences. You will understand people in a whole new way, realising our brains all work slightly differently and enabling you to appreciate and respect that we are all different. Do you know someone who seems to always talk faster than you? Does the waiter or waitress seem to be on another time scale: too slow or even too fast but never realising it? Do you answer a ringing phone so quickly it surprises the caller? You may be hearing sound slightly faster. The analogies are endless once you have a clear understanding of this theory. Right now, from this very *moment of awareness*, you will notice a whole new world. You will see things you never noticed before in people and understand them clearly. And it will change you forever. You will become much more empathetic and your humility will become limitless.

Understanding Autism continued

An abundance of information at the subconscious level, when not being sorted for relevancy to the situation with the rest being disposed of, will cause an overflow of data onto the conscious awareness. Your conscious mind will literally be drowning in data, suffocating you in information, effectively slowing the world down around you. During such a moment an autistic child will hear every word of every conversation around him, smell every fruit on every shelf, see every move of every motion, and feel the wind pushing him. It's like time is standing still, being frozen up in the moment.

Asperger's Syndrome, on the other hand, is the transformation of a normal set of high-definition conscious moments into only a few super-enhanced moments of awareness, with the individual being oblivious to anything else for that duration. This is an explanation I am writing an entire book on; for those interested please follow our Facebook page ImAutisticToo.

Biological signatures of Autism: a larger-than-normal head

Why brain size is more significant than thought

A baby's brain at birth is around half the size of an adult's brain. As such the baby's mind would encapsulate time to last twice as long as that of his parent and therefore would perceive each and every movement, every single sound and every touch to be lasting twice as long, hence everything is very slow in the mind of the baby. For more on this, read Autism and Head Size Study. When the brain of an autistic child develops too quickly, the whole scenario around him changes. Everything around him, which was supposed to be transpiring at a very slow rate enabling him to follow through, is now happening way too fast for him to comprehend, literally stripping precious time from his mind. Our every move, sound and even touch would become no less than terrifying for his now almost adult mind, a mind still in dire need of the relevant data and know how to help him make sense of the world around him.

Autism and Solutions

I believe there is much that can be done to rectify time perception simply by knowing how to manipulate awareness of time and steering it in the right direction. This can be achieved by means of virtual realities and the administration of very precise doses of task-specific drugs directly related to the metabolic rates to bridge this problem during the important developmental stages. Some of the work of Bill Mueller is directly addressing issues with over sensitivity to sound. It is my deepest intention to open up new ideas to help solve the struggles related with Autism.

Some of the many research studies supporting this theory

It is generally considered that the sensory inflow to the neural system is cut into fragments, which then are bound to each other, based on their features, to result in sensory perception. This idea is supported by flicker-fusion of visual images, when perception of continuous movement might be provided by a series of fixed visual frames.

(Ruben Tikidji-Hamburyan and Witali Dunin-

Congress of <u>Neuroinformatics</u>)

"Publicly announced in September 2013 Research led by Trinity University of Dublin in collaboration with a few other universities announced a remarkable discovery relating to the perceptions of time amongst the animal kingdom of which humans certainly are no exclusion." <u>Flicker Fusion Frequencies</u>

The pillars upon which my theory is based

No man has, nor ever will, be capable of any profound discovery no matter how small, without having trampled upon the hard built foundations constructed from the blood, sweat and tears of others. Not even Einstein could claim otherwise.

Only by gaining a fundamental understanding of time, space and energy, based on pure logical reasoning, will you be capable of understanding what the true realities of the present, past and future really entail, being responsible for our perceived realities. Any one moment of awareness can never consist of anything less than an equal duration of the present, past and future, no matter how long or short that duration might be.

Take careful note of the following statement, which is fundamental in getting to understand the true realities of our existence, especially if you eventually want to gain a complete understanding of Autism.

The only way possible to see into the future is by living in the past in which the present moment has already occurred.

Only by coming to understand this is it possible to understand the true nature of our realities. The transitional gates of our minds are responsible for the transformation of consciousness into any one single moment of awareness, in which the metabolic rate plays a critical role.

It is these transitional gates which are responsible for safeguarding us from the harsh realities of our physical interaction at the subconscious level, constrained to a different level of time perception.

Yet these transitional gates, for various reasons, are quite often compromised, causing all types of phenomena, resulting in the likes of Autism, Asperger's, ADHD, sleep paralysis, déjà vu, bipolar disorders, multiple personalities, schizophrenia, seizures and the list goes on.

In Conclusion

Although our realities are not that difficult to understand, there certainly is much more to be learned to gain a clear understanding of them.

What you, the reader, have been exposed to so far is merely a taste of what our realities consist of. There are numerous mind-blowing facts that will change the way you think and behave forever, for once the door is opened it can never be closed.

A Message from Clayton

Bushy Van Eck has spent his entire adult life working on his theory. Although being ignored by some, he has never given up hope to share his theory. Bushy was born and raised in Brakpan, South Africa. The school systems of the 1960s and 1970s in South Africa had no place for a gifted child. What he has been especially ridiculed for, even until this day, is his very poor handwriting skills (writing he can mostly not even read himself). Bushy took on a normal life and a normal job until the internet allowed him to become self-taught in Physics and much more. I have had the privilege of studying and learning his theory. If you have read books like "The Secret", "The Law of Attraction" and hundreds of other self-help books but still feel something is missing, Bushy's work can help fill that gap.

Bushy is honoured to be included this summer in the filming of the "US Autism Road Tour". There are no words that can express our gratitude to all the supporters, especially those affected by Autism. No theory that can expand our understanding of Autism should be ignored, for that could be an injustice to those who need it the most.

Please give Bushy your support by following our Facebook page ImAutisticToo.

Contact Info:

Bushy: bushy@prisonersofourminds.co.za

For inquiries on lectures, speaking engagements, etc. in the US please contact Clayton:

claytonulrich@gmail.com.

Thank you

Be sure to watch out for Bushy's upcoming book

A list of the best Asperger's movies

Here is our list of the best movies on Asperger's Syndrome and Autism. These are all movies we have enjoyed watching in the past and have found many of them very moving and inspirational. We hope you enjoy them too.

"Adam" – rated PG13

"<u>Adam</u>" is a brilliant love story that debuted in 2009 and takes place in bustling New York City. The movie is about Adam's life as a shy and lonesome man with Asperger's Syndrome. Actor Hugh Dancy stars as Adam and his keen abilities as a performer shine through as he portrays Adam with very real and believable Asperger's mannerisms. Dancy's performance draws the viewer in to understand Adam's plight as he meets and develops a friendship with his new neighbour, a pretty kindergarten teacher named Beth, played by Rose Byrne. Adam struggles to communicate with Beth and often finds it easier to recite interesting facts that he knows about various subjects, including his favourite, space exploration. Adam knows everything about astronomy in detail and his knowledge intrigues Beth. Through their many awkward and often comical moments, a meaningful relationship unfolds between Adam and Beth.

Adam

"My Name is Khan" – not rated

The movie "My Name is Khan" is a story that became undone after September 11, 2001. The United States changed rapidly after the terrorist assault, and much of the country became fearful of Muslim people. Rizvan Khan, played by actor Shah Rukh Khan, is originally a Muslim from India. He is a gentle person who endures the difficulties caused by Asperger's Syndrome. Until that fateful day, Rizvan lives a somewhat normal life in America. He meets and marries a Hindu woman named Mandira, played by Kajol Devgan. They create a good life together, but once Mandira's son becomes a victim of an attack on Muslims, she sends Rizvan away. The remainder of the movie finds Rizvan on a quest to make things right and win back his wife. "My Name Is Khan" sends a message of open-mindedness to the world and sheds some light on understanding both the difficulties of Asperger's and the sometimes ominous Muslim ways.

"Mozart and the Whale" – rated PG13"Mozart & The Whale" is based on the book about the lives of Jerry and Mary Newport, two adults who fell in love and are each affected with Asperger's Syndrome. In the movie, the couple is Donald, played by Josh Hartnett, and Isabella, played by Radha Mitchell. The two become acquainted through a group Donald creates for autistic adults to interact with each other and to help prevent the loneliness that often occurs for people with Asperger's. As the two become a couple, they grapple with their differences in daily social situations and learn various coping methods. Donald and Isabella each possess unique talents, but the difficulties of their pasts give them something in common that helps create a strong bond between them.

The actors do an excellent job of portraying the couple. The story is well written, believable and, at the same time, it gives the audience a new understanding of the fact that everyone faces challenges in life. "Mozart and the Whale" was filmed in 2004 in the heart of Spokane, Washington. The movie highlights the beauty of the city and its special attractions. It is a 'must see' movie for anyone interested in Asperger's Syndrome.

<u>Mozart & The Whale (Widescreen)</u>

"Temple Grandin" – rated PG

"Temple Grandin" is the real life story of Temple Grandin. It illustrates her struggle with Autism and her subsequent achievements in life. Not only did Temple find a way to overcome the emotional distress, but she also gained a Ph.D. in animal science and became an internationally recognised speaker in the autistic community. Inspired by generations of people diagnosed with Autism, <u>Temple Grandin</u> is truly an example to us all.

"Little Man Tate" – rated PG

"<u>Little Man Tate</u>" came out in 1991. It is about a young genius who has some Asperger's traits and his single, loving, hard-working, and very protective mother. The child is Fred Tate, played by Adam Hann-Byrd. He has the ability to solve complex math problems in his mind and is an expert piano player. Fred gets nervous when too many adults give him attention and he depends on the sheltering of his mum, Dede, played by actress, and the "Little Man Tate" director, Jodie Foster.

As Fred's obvious talents gain more attention, a child psychologist who owns a school for gifted children enters the picture. She tries to pressure Dede to enrol Fred in her school but Dede struggles because she knows her child and puts major importance on Fred's life being lived as normally as possible.

"Little Man Tate" is a story about triumph over adversity. The characters learn wonderful things about themselves and each other. The movie looks at the life of a young child prodigy and determines how to find a healthy balance in a world that can sometimes be less than kind to those who are different.

"I Am Sam" – Rated PG13

"I Am Sam" is an emotionally powerful movie about the love between a parent and his child. Actor Sean Penn is Sam Dawson, a developmentally disabled single father who is raising his little daughter, Lucy, played by Dakota Fanning. The child's mother abandoned them shortly after Lucy's birth, but Sam has done an excellent job of loving and caring for his daughter. Sam also has a marvellous support group of mentally challenged friends and a neighbour woman that help him care for Lucy.

As Lucy gets older and is attending school, she begins to realise that her daddy is different from the other daddies and she understands that he has learning disabilities. The other children tease her, but Lucy and Sam have a strong and loving bond that is unshakable. The authorities enter the picture and eventually move Lucy to a foster home, where they feel she will receive better care, but Sam and Lucy will not have it.

As Sam prepares to fight for custody of his daughter, he seeks help from attorney Rita Harrison, played by Michelle Pfeiffer. Each of the actors delivers exceptional performances and "I Am Sam" sends out an overwhelming message of the power of unconditional love. The music soundtrack, which is comprised of favourite Beatles tunes, offers a delightful addition for moviegoers.

Asperger's, Violence and the Adam Lanza Shootings in CT

In the wake of the recent shootings by Adam Lanza at Sandy Hook Elementary School in Newtown, CT, there had been a lot of speculation that it may have stemmed from the fact that Adam Lanza had Asperger's Syndrome. Because of this there is a lot of fear that people are going to think that all Aspies are gun-slinging killers, and many parents are concerned that their children may face discrimination because of the issue.

I thought I would write a short post as we had a few requests from people on our mailing list to comment on this issue.

Firstly, we would like to say that when something like this happens, there is a tendency for the press to sensationalise events. People look for something or someone to blame. The conclusions that are often made in this time don't necessarily stand up. In a blog by John Elder Robison, he raises the point that correlation does not imply causation. In the same way that just because most of the gun-related violence is performed by

Caucasian males, that doesn't make all Caucasian males killers.

Secondly, while there is research to suggest that people on the Autism Spectrum have a slightly higher rate of aggressive behaviour and outbursts, it is a kind of behaviour that is not characterised by premeditated attempts at mass murder. Examining crime statistics, also, we can see that the violent crime rate for adults with Asperger's is 1.3%, compared to 1.25% in the population as a whole. Also, if we examine deeper into the statistics we can see that the majority of these kinds of offenses (those perpetrated by Aspies) are actually related to property offences.

Thirdly, it's unclear whether Adam had actually been formally diagnosed with Asperger's. Psychologist Dr Beth Weiner recently commented that studies of the behaviour of Adam seem to indicate that it's more likely he had an antisocial personality disorder than Asperger's. According to Dr Weiner, "If you bump into someone with Asperger's in the hallway, they might not process it correctly and they might lash out, but they don't plan out something in a premeditated way."

One thing very clear about the whole event is that both Adam and his mother clearly had a few issues that were also unrelated to Asperger's. We hope that the media eventually sees sense in the wake of this incident. It's not fair to discriminate against an entire group of people just because of the actions of one individual.

The Impact of an Asperger's Parent on a Family

by Cynthia Kim

Having a parent with Asperger's in the family can be a mixed bag. Aspie parents tend to be unconventional. This can mean anything from having an unusual way of expressing love to being the kind of parent who will spend weeks helping his/her child build a scale model replica of the Island of Sodor out of Lego.

The effect of an Asperger's parent on a family may be positive or negative, but most likely it will be some of each. At times, in two-parent households, the parent who isn't on the spectrum will need to step in and help out in areas where the Aspie parent struggles. Of course, the Aspie parent can return the favour by helping out in areas of his/her own strength. Children often figure out early on that Dad is better at helping with maths homework and more fun to watch sci-fi shows with, while Mum is better at kissing boo-boos and giving friendship advice. This happens naturally in most families; it just may be a little more pronounced in families where one parent has Asperger's.

Beyond their personal strengths and weaknesses, parents with Asperger's face some natural hurdles that can impact a family:

Sensory sensitivities: Aspies can be sensitive to certain types of light, noise, or smells. With children in the house, limiting things like the sound of the television, the level of noise during a play date or the smells that a baby produces can be difficult. It may be helpful for the Aspie parent to have a quiet place they can escape to when necessary to regroup or to divide up family responsibilities to accommodate the Aspie partner's sensitivities.

Social communication deficits: social communication is a big part of parenting. At home, parents are constantly communicating with their children, whether it's to discipline them, to let them know that they're loved or to explain a difficult homework assignment. Away from home, children rely on their parents to advocate for them at school and show them how to get along in the world. When a parent struggles in this area, it may be necessary for them to seek assistance, either from their partner or another trusted family member.

Household management: executive function difficulties can make it hard for Aspies to stay organised themselves, let alone keep a household of three or more people running smoothly. Many families with a parent on the spectrum rely heavily on organisational aids like family calendars, reminder lists and routines to stay on track.

Love and support: Aspies often have an unusual way of showing love and bonding with others. For example, many people on the spectrum are naturally drawn to practical gestures of love and support, such as solving a problem or doing something helpful for a loved one. If a child finds it difficult to understand an Aspie parent's bonding style (or any aspect of their parenting), it may help for both parents to explain that mummy/daddy's brain is wired differently and that's why they do X instead of Y.

On the upside, many parents with Asperger's find that they make great parents. Aspies are known for being loyal, honest, and non-judgmental with strong values and an independent spirit. Being raised in a family that is somewhat non-traditional, children of Aspie parents often grow up to be open-minded, independent thinkers who are tolerant of other people's differences.

Often, the effect that an Aspie parent has on a family is largely dependent on how the family sees Asperger's. Both parents can set a positive example for the family by treating Asperger's as a natural difference that requires everyone to make some adaptations. As the family grows and ages, those adaptations may change, and in time, they may become so natural that everyone will forget that their family isn't quite the same as other families.

Asperger's and Flexibility

By Paddy Joe Moran

Structure is obviously an incredibly important part of most autistic people's lives. Without some level of structure and routine most autistic people would be unable to cope. Of course there are different levels of this, and some people are much more able to be flexible than others. A structured routine can be essential for autistic people in allowing them to cope with day-to-day life, improving their organisational skills, and helping them avoid stress and outbursts. But life cannot be one long structured routine, and there must be some level of flexibility in everybody's life.

Flexibility is hard for people with autism, but everybody who is autistic should at least try to be as flexible as they can — depending on what level of capacity they have. This doesn't mean abandoning any structure and routine, it simply means trying to allow some flexibility into that routine. Somebody may have a plan for their week, and they may wish to stick to that exactly. This could be fine for a few weeks, or even a few months, but at some point someone they have planned to see, for example, may become ill, or have an accident, and obviously there is no way around this — the autistic person's plans will have to change.

AUTISM AND FLEXIBILITY

It's not easy, but there are ways of dealing with flexibility and change. One way is to have a chart that details what you are doing for the week, but include in this something that reminds you that things may change — maybe put an extra note next to things that you know are more likely to be cancelled or changed. Try to include some flexible time within your chart; so you might just structure a couple of periods in every day or so where you just do whatever you feel like — if you struggle with this level of spontaneity then you can write a little list of things to choose from. This idea gives you more freedom if you do need to rearrange something on the chart, while keeping the stress level down. Also, having a *script or a *sketch that you can read and look at if things do change is helpful because it can calm you down in the moment. It might not stop you getting stressed, but it might help you to calm down faster. You can also come up with a plan B beforehand; i.e. say to yourself "This is what we are planning, but if something changes we will do that instead." Also, talk about change and flexibility to the people you are likely to be making plans with, and try to make sure that they know not to make definite plans with you if they are not sure they will be able to stick to them. Tell people that you would rather they didn't make any plans than make a plan they think they'll probably have to change. Try to be aware of certain things in advance; for example, if you are supposed to be going on a day out with your family, but for the entire evening before it's been pouring with rain, you might think to yourself that the activity may well be cancelled because of the bad weather.

Thinking for yourself instead of being entirely

reliant on what others may decide is a good way of becoming more flexible.

There is also the issue of bigger and smaller changes — some changes such as school/work holidays and Christmas we know are coming, and are therefore much more easy to plan for than smaller, day-to-day changes. A small change could be something as simple as going from week-day to week-end mode — and vice versa — or simply being unable to have a meal at your regular time; things that are unavoidable, and to most people minor, but which to a lot of autistic people could be incredibly distressing. Small changes can be just as difficult to deal with as large ones and can need just as much preparation — just because something appears small to a neurotypical person, it does not mean it is going to be small to an autistic person.

Even though flexibility and change are hard for people with Autism, they are inescapable facts of life. And if you are unable to be flexible at all, your life is going to be very difficult, and never really get any easier. Even though it is hard, and a lot of autistic people will never be entirely comfortable with being flexible, it is possible to make it that bit easier. Start by learning how to deal with planned changes, and as your confidence grows it will become easier to be more flexible when an unexpected change occurs.

*Learn more about Scripts & Sketches in my book "Helping Children with Autism Spectrum Conditions Through Everyday Transitions". Although the book is targeted at parents/children, the techniques can be adapted for autistic people of all ages who are struggling with transition, change, and flexibility.

Paperback edition http://jkp.com/catalogue/book/9781849052757

Kindle edition http://www.amazon.co.uk/Children-Spectrum-Conditions-Everyday-Transitions-ebook/dp/B00C4XR1PI/ref=sr_1_1?s=digital-text&ie=UTF8&qid=1407940141&sr=1-1&keywords=helping+children+with+autism+spectrum+conditions+through+everyday+transitions

Living on the wrong planet

By Paddy Joe Moran

Often people with Autism will feel completely out of place in society. Despite the fact that more and more people are being diagnosed as autistic, trying to go through life in a majority neurotypical world can feel almost like an impossible task for people with Autism.

There is a very simple way to explain to neurotypical people how it feels – simply switch it around. Imagine everybody you are dealing with on a day-to-day basis is autistic; the legal and social rules of your life are set, and enforced by people with Autism. Imagine that every relationship with people that you try to make is with somebody who has Autism. You might not understand large parts of their behaviour, and they definitely won't understand many of the things you say and do. This is how autistic people feel on a day-to-day basis; living in a world created, and mostly run, by neurotypical people.

I don't want this to be some kind of 'Poor me, I have Autism' article. This article is simply trying to explain the feelings a lot of autistic people live with. Autistic people grow up with a set of feelings and beliefs; a mindset, a view of the world and themselves, that simply isn't shared by a lot of people they know — even those closest to them for much of the time. Lots of autistic people are told that the way they think and feel is wrong. Neurotypical people are often told that it is good to be different, and stand out from the crowd; that it is good to have their own thoughts, and not just conform to what society wants. This might be true, but it is incredibly difficult when society might view an autistic person as rude or violent for behaving in a certain way.

People will make judgements for everything, however trivial — e.g. you don't laugh at somebody's joke because it's not funny, and they take a dislike to you. It's not like it's your fault that they can't tell a funny joke, but many neurotypical people are so insecure that they would rather you laughed, and lied to their face, and allow them to carry on deluding themselves that they are something they are not. Most autistic people don't need to do this. We know what we are. We might not always be happy with it, and some of us might even hate it but, by and large, we don't try and deny it. Even if some people are able to temper their autistic traits a bit to try to get by in society, they generally don't deny it to themselves, or to those closest to them. And in a way I think this is where a lot of the problems come from; insecure neurotypical people looking at somebody who is autistic, and has a perfect knowledge of who they are, and not understanding how somebody can be comfortable with the fact that they don't like to socialise, or that they don't bother to conform to social norms. Now I don't want to generalise — there will be autistic people who aren't comfortable with who they are, and there will be neurotypical people who are comfortable with themselves. Nor do I want to turn this into some kind of attack on neurotypical people — it's nothing to do with that. All I am trying to say is that it can be difficult going through life when you are told that the way you think, and the way you feel, is wrong. Even if you have complete confidence in yourself, the fact that everybody else thinks you have confidence in something that isn't right can be a difficult thing to deal with.

The phrase 'living on the wrong planet' is often used by people with Autism to describe how they feel about their place in the world. Everything is set up to make life easier for neurotypical people, which inadvertently makes it more difficult for people with Autism. Although some people with Autism will be able to cope, and find their way to get by in the world, no autistic person ever feels a hundred percent comfortable throughout their life. It's also worth neurotypical people remembering quite how alien their own behaviour might be to people with Autism. Despite having said all this, there is no reason why someone with Autism can't have a good and successful life, and find a way to get by in a world that mostly caters for neurotypical people.

Chapter 4- Solutions for Living with Asperger's

Mindset

This section is devoted to solutions and strategies you can use to improve your quality of life.

It's important you never give up on the dreams that you would like to achieve and activities that you would like to do because you think it's not possible. Many of the challenges those on the spectrum face can be overcome or solutions learned. Having the right mindset and being determined to achieve what you want, no matter how much work is involved, is a valuable asset.

It's not surprising people on the spectrum have low self-esteem.

Many times people on the spectrum are judged as being stupid, inattentive and lazy. This was certainly true for me. Never being able to measure up to the behavioural or academic expectations takes its toll. At school I battled with the easy stuff but was exceptional at the difficult parts, the parts that can only truly be perceived and understood by the visual thinker.

When I was taking my A level exams, which in England are the exams you take at 18 as a preparation for university, my parents had to have a difficult time talking to one of my tutors.

The school (teachers) accused me of not making an effort, not understanding the content and said I would probably fail to achieve basic grades. There was even talk of my parents having to pay the costs of taking the exam because I was expected to fail.

After the conversation I realised that even though I was following I was failing to communicate effectively what I understood. It forced me to learn more about better communication with NTs.

Exams are always a struggle with time and handwriting but that day I tried my best to make everything legible. When the time came to get my results I was in fear; I got called into a room by the tutor, who talked with my parents. He was really grim faced and serious looking and I suspected the worst. But the first words he uttered were ... "I have to apologise to you, Mark. I got you wrong. You have got an A grade. In fact you are the only one from this college to get such a grade. I was elated and came away from that encounter knowing I could actually achieve anything I wanted if only I could learn to apply my mind in the best way.

Part of the problem with AS is the prominence of so called abstract thoughts with pronounced difficulties in being able to crystalise those thoughts in clear language. This is the benefit and curse of the visual thinker.

One example of how I begin to leverage this relates to previous positions of working as an IT systems architect. Complex problems would be described to me that I would usually visualise in pictures and then scribble an abstract or diagram down on a coffee-stained piece of paper. No one could fully understand the design which would then take me many months to document and explain linguistically to NTs.

IT systems was the application I found for my gift but I know many others have been able to apply their gift in music, art, architecture, engineering and science. The challenge is working out how to find the best application for your mind.

Another example I can give from my own experience of not giving up is when I struggled for years to learn to drive because of motor difficulties and sensory issues. I failed my driving test seven times and was even told by one instructor that I would probably never pass my test. How many people would give up at that point? ... But not me. I knew driving would give me a sense of freedom and independence. I changed my instructor and began to learn new ways of driving.

A friend even suggested that I buy my own car so I could drive with the learner plates on with other friends who were qualified drivers. It helped get me in the right mindset until I hit another obstacle ... .

The night before my eighth test, my girlfriend at the time broke the news to me that she was leaving me for another guy because I was not emotionally available. I didn't sleep the whole night but realising that my day was about to get a whole lot worse if I failed again, I stood determined not to let that happen. The test that day was harder than any others but I stood by my resolve and determination to pass no matter what. On the eighth time I passed with flying colours.

Imagine the joy in me when I could drive to work that day after everything that had happened!

Mindset is everything, so I encourage you all no matter how difficult things get, never give up. Everything is possible.

Applying Mindfulness Strategies to Manage ADHD and Asperger's

By Sang H. Kim

Attention Deficit Hyperactivity Disorder is very common in people with Asperger's. In children with Asperger's, it is the most commonly diagnosed comorbid psychiatric condition. Nearly half of children diagnosed with an Autism Spectrum Disorder are also diagnosed with ADHD. Because both of these conditions persist into adulthood, it is likely that there are also a significant number of adults who have both AS and ADHD. While the strategies discussed in this guest post by Sang H. Kim are geared toward individuals with ADHD, they can also be applied to the impairments with executive function that many people with Asperger's experience.

Applying mindfulness strategies to manage ADHD

Even at the best of times, our minds naturally tend to wander, browsing for something more immediately pleasurable to settle on. For those

with Attention Deficit Hyperactivity
Disorder (ADHD), staying focused on one thing is
a daunting challenge unless the activity is
inherently rewarding.

However, in contrast to the inattention,
impulsivity and hyperactivity, which characterise
ADHD, individuals with ADHD also have the
unique capacity for super focus on what they love.
Unable to control their impulses, they move from
one thing to another, until they find something
that captivates their attention. Then they dive in,
with no fear of getting lost in time. Forgetting
everything else, they often miss deadlines at work
or school. Then the last-minute frenzy required to
get back on track exacerbates their already high
anxiety.

How mindfulness can help

Many people find that applying strategies from
mindfulness practice can help to reduce the
inattention, impulsivity and hyperactivity
characteristics of ADHD. Mindfulness can also
help when it comes to putting the strengths of
ADHD to work. Recognising and working with the
two contrasting characteristics of inattention and

super-focus can be a powerful way to positively manage ADHD symptoms.

Inattention, one of the core traits of ADHD, is a deficit in holding attention on a task. It diminishes our ability to put things together cohesively, to plan and to organise our behaviour.

Mindfulness, on the other hand, is simply paying attention to what you do. Being mindful can help to guide your attention to a specific activity, thought or feeling. It begins with recognising what is happening inside and around you, with openness and curiosity, nonjudgmentally. It is the ground zero, so to speak, from which your awareness builds.

Ideally, in that neutral state of mind, you can reflect on and discern habitual thought patterns and reactions, and choose alternatives to change impulsive behaviour. Choice is the key. However, for individuals with ADHD, reaching this neutral state can be hard. Beginning with simple strategies drawn from mindfulness practice can help to reduce distractions and draw on the ability to super-focus that most people with ADHD have.

Mindfulness strategies to promote focus

1. Develop attention anchors. Having a tangible way to bring your mind back to the present can help you stay on task. Taking a few deep breaths, clapping your hands or spending a minute pacing can all serve as ways to reanchor yourself in the present. Rather than trying to stop your attention from drifting, give yourself permission to wander off any time, enjoy a short diversion, and then use your anchor to bring yourself back to the present before the distraction derails you from your task.

2. Be aware of your needs. Stepping back and reframing a problem can help us get a fresh look at difficult issues. Often those with ADHD need to change the way they are approaching a challenging task. For example, if you have difficulty in understanding verbal instructions, ask for or use visual or written directions. If you find it hard to get back on task when interrupted, hang a *do not disturb* sign on your desk, cubicle or door. Identify your best working style and invite those around you to support it.

3. Pause before you act. A short time delay

between the occurrence of an idea and acting on that thought can reduce impulsivity and hyperactivity by creating a mental buffer zone. People with ADHD tend to generate many ideas and have difficulty following through. They end up with many half-finished projects, bouncing from one idea to the next. By taking a short timeout, you will find that you become more discriminating about acting on your ideas, which makes you more likely to complete the things you do start.

Mindfulness strategies that capitalise on ADHD traits

1. Take advantage of super-focus. People with ADHD have the ability to super-focus on activities that interest them. This ability can be an asset if you can harness it. When you find yourself in super-focus mode, enjoy what you are doing to the fullest, but be sure to stop on a positive note. This can be hard, because we have a tendency to drive ourselves to exhaustion in this mode. Instead, try to stop when you are feeling good about yourself. Doing so creates a positive behaviour pattern that is inherently rewarding and will increase your feelings of control while capitalising on your asset.

2. Use your strengths as an entry point. We all have responsibilities, whether for work, school or family. It can be very hard for people with ADHD to initiate activities that they have little interest in or find difficult, like certain types of homework or chores. Using your strengths can help to make initiation less difficult. For example, if you are a visual thinker, begin a homework project by creating the visual aspects of a report first and then writing the background once you get 'warmed up'. Or make a visual map of a project to help you organise your thoughts before you begin.

3. Use time to your advantage. Some people with ADHD work well in big chunks. Once they begin an activity, they are most productive if they can work for several hours uninterrupted. Others find that the pressure of a time limit helps them focus. For example, Elton John says that he never spends more than 40 minutes on composing a song because beyond that he gets bored. By knowing the limits of his attention, he can avoid the problems that arise from boredom, including distraction, poor productivity and a loss of creativity.

Being mindful does not necessarily mean that you will always be focused on the task at hand. Instead, it means that you are actively working to be aware of where your attention is and discovering ways to deliberately guide it to where you would like it to be. For individuals with ADHD, mindfulness can be a powerful strategy for engaging with the mind and getting to know ourselves better. Until we understand how we work best, it is impossible to begin developing strategies that work for us.

My top diet tips

I know we all hate to be told what is good to eat and I'm sure we all know what is good for us and what is not. But what I can honestly say is that diet has had one of the biggest impacts on my mental and physical state.

Eating healthy has enabled me to stay more focused and in control of all my emotions. Some great tips were mentioned previously in the book "Emotional Mastery For Adults with Asperger's" but I thought I would follow up with some diet and supplement tips that I use to keep optimal.

Super greens and the alkaline diet

There is growing evidence of how an alkaline diet helps us be more happy and allows our body to operate in a more optimal way. This involves eating more green alkaline plant-like foods as opposed to the acid foods that the modern diet consists of (french fries, fried food, meat and snacks).

The best way to ensure an alkaline diet is to eat more green foods, but with the modern diet, this is not always possible. What I do to supplement my diet is to take one of the many green super foods into my diet. Although there are many others, here is a link to one of the supplements I use http://aspergerstestsite.com/supergreens.

Omega 3

Omega 3 is one of the supplements we can take to enhance clarity in our minds. It also helps to reduce the effects of depression that many on the spectrum suffer from.

There are many kinds of Omega 3; it can be found in high quantities in fish oil or in flax seed oil. I have experimented with a few different kinds, including fish oil supplements, Udo's Choice (http://www.aspergerstestsite.com/Udos) and, in particular, Krill oil http://www.aspergerstestsite.com/krill. The thing I like about krill oil is that it is more readily absorbed by the body than fish oil. Udo's Choice can be a good choice if one is vegetarian, although it becomes less effective if the body is regularly introducing caffeine into the system.

One thing one needs to bear in mind is the source of the fish or krill oil, because the oceans have become increasingly toxic and, in particular, the Pacific is becoming highly radioactive following the Fukushima radioactive disaster. I try to avoid all fish products from the Pacific. I believe it's only a matter of time before the serious health impacts of this disaster are known.

Know your blood type

All of our bodies are different and have different needs when it comes to nutrition. I am a big fan of dieting by blood type. I know my body needs to eat meat but that is not the same for everyone. When I don't eat meat and, in particular, red meat I tend to get quite pale and have low energy levels.

I would advise everyone to find out what blood type you are and structure your diet around that. You can find out more about the diet that is most fitting for your blood type at http:// www.dadamo.com/.

Avoid toxic food sources

Many say genetically modified food is responsible for increases in Autism and I personally think there is a lot of truth in this. However, the impact of toxins in our diet is huge, leading to many problems that we cannot immediately see. I know we don't always have the choice financially to eat organic foods but if you try it for a month you will notice a big difference in your moods.

Avoid comfort foods

Now I know this is going to make a few people unhappy. We all like to eat comfort food, but very often this leads us to being in a bad mood in the long run. Sugar and acid foods give us a temporary good feeling but then leave us feeling worse than we did before. If you have not seen the movie "Super Size Me", I recommend watching it. The full version can be found here:

https://www.youtube.com/watch?v=8GA8LnPg4ZA.

Aspies and diet

By Robert Laing

Aspies don't like change and they especially don't like change in their foods. Favourite foods are bland and come at the same time of the same day, week in, week out, come what may. Any of this sounding familiar so far? Studies have shown that among the favourite foods of Aspies are wheat-based things like bread and pasta, cereals, and, above all, milk. That about describes my own diet down to a tee. Or the basis of it, anyway. I couldn't stomach fruit growing up and I was very wary of anything new, no matter how much Mum and Dad said I might like it. Macaroni, lasagna, even spaghetti all featured heavily in my childhood diet, as they do for most Aspies. Well-cooked but bland flavours. I was bored. I was told that other things like fruit, salads and so forth were better for me. I could not, then, however, stomach many of the contrasting and sometimes either all-too-sweet or all-too-bitter tastes or flavours that these things brought with them.

Texture is a real issue for me, as well as many other Aspies, from the research I have done. And first of all, the bad news — there is no 'one size fits all' easy cure answer. My own best way around it is to take things slowly. It will be frightening and daunting at first but the pay-off at the end is fantastic. My own way around it was to mix the tastes. See what it was (and is) that other people like so much about the food you see them eating. This is also a very good way to start and develop social skills — eating as a social thing. I found that as I was trying a new thing it helped greatly to be with someone, to have someone to talk to, both around and about the food, because it took my mind, slowly, off the fact that I was doing something I really did not, at least initially, want to do. It will be a slow process, and the key here for parents, carers, friends, whoever, is **not** to force the change upon you, as the Aspie. Create a warm atmosphere, a relaxed place in which you can both eat and just talk about whatever. Comments such as "How are you finding that?", "Isn't this nice?", "What is it you're liking about your meal?" and so on and so forth will help draw the Aspie out of him/herself and increase his/her confidence in both the areas of adapting to new things and also being active socially.

What we will look at here are some short steps towards changing the diet of an Aspie, the reasons why we, as Aspies, should do so and the benefits (both long- and short-term) which will be had from doing so.

I know I very soon started to feel better after introducing fruit into my diet. I felt much more active both mentally and physically. Yes, I liked my bread. Yes, I liked my milk. Yes, I liked (and still very much do like) lots of wheat-based foods. But they are bland foods, which never change and that is the real reason, I believe, why we Aspies like them. Harsh though it may seem, all recommendations for change made here are for the benefit of both the Aspie and those who care about them.

How does diet tie in with repetitive behaviours? The Aspie is the ultimate creature of habit. We are used to eating at a particular time (or times) each day. We are used to eating particular things every day or at certain times of the week. When we get something new or unexpected, for us it is scary, unless handled in a certain way. The overarching advice to get over this fear of the new would seem to be, introduce it gradually. Two familiar things for (or with) every one new thing would be my advice, drawn from experience. That way, we are getting the repetition as well as the new thing.

I had, as a child (and still do have), great difficulties with new textures. Where most people can simply put some food in their mouths, chew quickly and be done with it, I could spend what seemed like hours chewing on the same piece of food. I had to know there were no nasty surprises waiting therein for me. I had to feel every inch of the food and know what I was getting into. Everyone else loved the surprise and the exploration of the new. I, on the other hand, did not. What this led to was boring familiarity.

Familiarity breeds a kind of comfort and what does comfort mean for the Aspie and non-Aspie alike? That's right: comfort food. Aspies, many studies have shown, love their comfort food. This is because, unlike the outside world, there are no horrific surprises to be had when you know what you are going to get to eat.

Websites such as www.autism.org.uk are a great help to parent/partner and Aspie alike in understanding this. Their suggestion of the creation of a food diary, for practical monitoring and change introduction purposes was a huge help to me among others, as it makes change manageable.

And manageability's the key word here. My own parents and others, good though their intentions were, tried to introduce new foods to me in the same way that one would with a so-called 'normal' child. The results were often nothing short of disastrous. And no-one, least of all me, knew why!

The reasons now, looking back, are obvious. It was new. I was scared. No-one had told me what to expect because no-one thought that they would have to do so. This was thirty years ago and more. People knew little about Autism, as we know it now. They knew absolutely nothing about Asperger's Syndrome. They just thought that I, and millions like me, were awkward, badly behaved children.

My parents had, when I was between the ages of about 4 and 15, to really persevere to get me to eat things like fruit. This again comes down to texture and sudden explosions of taste. I hated it, for example, when I put my teeth into an apple for the first time, piercing the skin (which didn't taste of much so that was fine, so far so good), and then the juice of the main fruit suddenly exploded into my mouth. Apart from anything else, I have very sensitive teeth and it really hurt, which made me scream. More frustration and lack of understanding from my parents. I went back to liking food with bland flavours. I was very jealous of people who could handle more.

My parents must, eventually, have decided that it was pointless getting me to try new things like fruit. It is interesting to note that one of the sources I consulted for this article (www.bbc.co.uk) mentions that Aspies like milk and milk-based food a lot.

Even now, I drink enough milk to give farmers a very healthy profit margin each year! But I just ate and drank the same things because that was what I did, that was all I felt able to do. But change frightened me, so what to do about it? The answer eventually came to me one day, while preparing my lunch for college. I was making the same kind of sandwich filling that I did every day. OK, the sandwich was made, what about stuff to go with it?

A bowl of fruit lay on the kitchen table. In it, an

apple and an orange. Bitterness and sweetness —
the extremes of which no normal food eater could
ever taste. What should I choose? But then, I had
a thought — why choose? Why not have both?
Only one of each, but hey, small steps, surely
taken.

Come lunchtime, I found out. Sandwiches with
egg mayonnaise, one of my favourite fillings. Then
the apple. My heart was going like a kick drum.
What happened next?

This time there was no explosion inside my
mouth. My teeth didn't feel as though they had
been hit by blasts of ice jets travelling at 90 miles
per hour. Just instead, a sweet, slow trickle of
flavour. It was really quite pleasant.

It occurred to me then that some things can work
in reverse also. Some foods which I (apparently)
liked as a baby, I cannot stand in adult life. I used
to have a banana every morning as a baby. Now,
even the smell of them makes me feel sick. Apples
and oranges; where once I hated, now I love them!

I made a note, from then, and for quite a while
afterwards, of every time something like this
happened to me. Or, more precisely, every time

that I **made** something like this happen. Not a food diary, exactly, but I think it is very important to keep some record of one's progress.

The only way to conquer your fears is to confront them. Do it one step at a time and you will soon notice a change in yourself.

Since introducing new foods into my diet, I have felt a lot better both physically and mentally. Aspies always want to feel better mentally, whether they classify it like this or not. The key to helping yourself start on this path is to give your body the correct fuel. People will go on at you about this, but in this case they have a definite point.

So, to sum up then, what did I learn from making changes to my diet? Well, you will get much more enjoyment out of your food. It will also give you many more ways in which to relate to those around you, both family and friends. You will also feel so much better, both physically AND mentally. You may think you are content now but just you wait until the changes in your diet kick in!

How to go about making that change? Start off by making a note of the foods you eat most regularly and what you want to get out of them, in terms of nourishment and enjoyment. Then, go to your doctor for a checkup. (What weight are you now? What is your ideal weight? What are you eating now which is good for you? What do you need to cut down on? What other foods could you try instead?)

Create a food diary detailing what you have eaten every day and how this has made you feel. An example of how to do this can be found on the www.autism.org.uk website. This will both enable you to track your progress and also really tell you what is working for *you*. This will also be very helpful for parents/carers/social workers etc. because it forms a record of progress in real time. It also keeps you on track as you will keep asking yourself two very important questions, namely: "Where am I?" and "Where do I want to be?". And it'll give you the motivation to get there!

Don't worry too much at the start about overeating. Remember, this is a *journey not a race*. If you try cutting out your comfort foods completely, you will only want them more. If you factor them into your food diary and your diet plan, you will enjoy them all the more. Think about what other activities you associate with food (watching TV, playing computer games and so forth). Try and do a little less eating when you are doing these every day. You will, as I do now, enjoy each of these activities so much more and, even better, you will soon stop associating them with food!

Certain foods made me feel good once upon a time. Now the fact that I am in control of a far more varied and interesting diet makes me feel even better. This is your life. This is your journey. Start now and enjoy!

Sleep

I, like many others on the spectrum, suffer from sleep problems. I think there are several reasons for this:

Anxiety

As discussed previously, adults with Asperger's are much more likely to suffer from anxiety; anxiety in turn leads to restless nights. In my other book, "Emotional Mastery for Adults for Asperger's", we look into the causes of anxiety for adults with Asperger's and what can be done about it. In essence, adults with Asperger's are generally carrying a lot of stress hormones, which is fuelled by the anxiety in their lives. These stress hormones make it very difficult to sleep.

Obsessive behaviour

The obsessive nature of those on the spectrum often creates a situation where the mind does not want to stop. The bounds of creativity and determination to solving problems can lead one to spend many a late night trying to figure out solutions.

Having explored the issue in myself for some time now, I can give a list of things that have worked for me.

- Stop using the computer 2 hours before bed

- Meditation

- Melatonin

- Magnesium

- Use of sleep apps

- Reduce caffeine intake

- Reduce stress

- Exercise

Stop using the computer 2 hours before bed

Like many on the spectrum I am addicted to technology, using the computer to work late into the night or even checking my iPhone using twitter and Facebook. All of the above stimulate dopamine, which gives the body a pleasure response and becomes addictive — thus stimulating the brain and preventing the rapid onset of sleep. Check out this article in "Psychology Today" about the relationship between Facebook and dopamine: http://www.psychologytoday.com/blog/the-beauty-prescription/201205/facebook-and-your-brain.

If you want to ensure you get a good night's rest, try and discipline yourself to stay away from your computer for two hours before bed. Instead, read a book, take a bath or even meditate.

Meditation

Meditation is a process where you begin becoming mindful of the thoughts that are prevalent in the brain. There are many different techniques to this, including becoming mindful of the inhalation and exhalation of the breath or staring into a candle. Meditating before bedtime brings the mind into a more still space.

Melatonin

Melatonin is a hormone which is manufactured from your brain's pineal gland. It is what tells your body when it's time to rest and when it's time to wake. Naturally, melatonin levels should rise when it begins to get dark and reduce in the morning, towards dawn. Due to our modern lifestyles, stress and an overactive brain, often this hormone does not get manufactured as it should. Being able to take an additional supplement at night, before bed gives signals to our body that it's time to rest. While it isn't a magic bullet in itself, it can be effective when used in conjunction with the other techniques mentioned.

Magnesium

Magnesium is one of the minerals that a lack of in the body will prevent sleep. Taking magnesium regularly as a supplement allows the body's relaxation mechanism to kick in.

Use of sleep apps

I have had good results with using sleep apps to get to sleep. By playing relaxing music or by using affirmations, these apps can really help you get to sleep easily.

The ones I have been using are:

Omvana: http://www.omvana.com/

Dormio: http://www.dormioapp.com/

Sleep app: https://itunes.apple.com/gb/app/
sleep-app-insomnia-relaxing/id585606271?mt=8.

Reduce caffeine intake

Yes, I know some of you will hate me for
suggesting this one, but caffeine is contributing to
your insomnia. Not only that but when you wake
up tired, the first thing you will do is reach for a
large cup of coffee to wake yourself up.

This, in turn, leads to you not being able to sleep.
Caffeine gives you a short buzz; it causes the body
to dig deep into its energy reserves and give you a
bit more energy, but when the buzz is over you
end up more tired than you were before. It also
leads to an increase in stress hormones and, even
though your body is exhausted, you will not be
able to sleep.

So do yourself a favour, either cut out caffeine
altogether or limit it to 2 cups per day. I know it's
hard but it is required.

I have found a good alternative to coffee is Mate;

this gives you a nice little wakeup but you don't experience the crash in the same way as you would with coffee. Check it out: http://en.wikipedia.org/wiki/Mate_%28beverage%29.

Reduce stress

We keep coming around to the effects of stress on sleep, but it is important. Being able to eliminate the causes of stress in our lives will have a great benefit on getting a good night's sleep. While it is easy for me to say "relax" (and, really, I know it isn't that easy), having a constant mindset about finding some time for ourselves each day to relax is one of the best gifts we can give ourselves. Relaxation is different for everyone but maybe a hot bath, listening to some relaxing music or maybe just even going for a work can be very beneficial.

Exercise

One thing I know in myself is that there is a very strong correlation between my lack of exercise and the amount of stress and restlessness in sleep I experience. When I exercise, I am more relaxed generally and find it much easier to sleep at night.

For me, exercise can take the form of going for a run in the morning, doing Qi Gong or yoga. I had quite a revelation in my life when I discovered bikram yoga. It is basically yoga in a sauna. Yes, that's right, high intensity workout in the form of yoga. If I force myself to do this after work, even though I am tired, it relaxes my mind and tires my body. As long as I don't get back into the pattern of going back on the computer immediately after I am almost guaranteed to sleep well (note, don't do this form of yoga if you are pregnant as the foetus is very sensitive to heat).

In conclusion, then, I would like to say that there are many methods for getting a better night's sleep. Some of these tips will resonate with you and others won't. It's important you find your own ways that work for you.

The world of dating and relationships

A common thread among adults with Asperger's is difficulty creating and maintaining meaningful romantic relationships, particularly with those considered neurotypical (NT). Some 'experts' even claim that 'true' people with Asperger's do not desire, and are incapable of, romantic relations. However, I disagree. Relationships for adults with Asperger's simply require more work, knowledge, and understanding.

Meeting a new partner and maintaining any kind

of relationship can be especially challenging for someone with AS because of the very traits that characterise Asperger's disorder.

For example:

• Difficulty reading social cues often makes conversation and interaction awkward.

• Difficulty intuiting emotions of others and responding appropriately is often perceived as coldness or lack of desire to connect.

• Tendency to expound on favourite hobbies or topics may come across as narcissistic or, worse, dull. Yet the Aspergian may never realise that the audience is bored.

• Strict adherence to rituals impacts flexibility for dating in general and the individual's availability to a new partner.

• Delayed adolescence, misunderstanding of sexual signals, and sensory issues can lead to the problem of expressing too much (or too little) affection.

If the situation seems hopeless, it need not. Plenty of people with AS have successfully navigated the world of dating and so can you. The following tips may help but are only starting points:

• Know yourself by embracing your diagnosis. This doesn't mean fixate on the label; simply read about Asperger's and high-functioning Autism to discover which traits and coping mechanisms may apply to you.

• Know yourself by studying your own behaviour. What are your mannerisms? Do you tend to lecture others about your favourite topic while they yawn and look away? Do you make an attempt to keep eye contact during conversations? Do you have difficulty with personal space and stand uncomfortably close to others in a group? If you aren't sure, ask those who know you best.

• Know others by studying both the NTs around you and in popular culture.

• Role play. Engage a friend, family member, or another Aspie to help you develop a dating 'script' to follow. Practise words, gestures, and even facial expressions that denote interest, concern, joy, etc.

• Consider therapy, if possible. A therapist specialising in Autism and adult Asperger's can guide you through cognitive behaviour therapy (CBT) and social skills training.

• Look for realistic and appropriate places to meet someone with similar interests or values. If you don't enjoy dancing or drinking, don't go bar-hopping to find a date. Try a meet-up group aimed at your interests, a support group, your church, or even an online dating site for AS.

• Communication. It is up to you whether or not you 'come out' to your date and the appropriate timing of that. If you do, be sure to provide accurate information so he or she can learn about your diagnosis.

• Don't wait for your soul mate to come along before dating. Instead, view each date as practice, or even a social experiment, a chance to test the skills or social theories you have managed to work out so far.

Dating can be difficult for anyone. For the person with AS, it can feel like a nightmare. However, with the right strategies in mind, it can be done successfully.

Chapter 5 — Personal Stories

Personal Stories Part 1 — Nancy

My name is Nancy. I'm 70 years old. Ever since I started hearing about Asperger's Syndrome, I've wondered if that was my problem. I have a very high IQ, especially in non-verbal areas, and I've lived with some intense social anxiety. When I took your test a few months ago, I scored on the low end of the AS. I believe it was 33.

I remember clearly when I stopped looking people in the eye. I was maybe 3 or 4. When I looked in people's eyes, I saw the anger, hatred, selfishness, and other negative feelings there. People don't all engender negative feelings, but what I saw really frightened me. So I stopped looking. I looked at their mouths instead to focus on what they were saying and not at their eyes to see what they were feeling. Just in the past couple of years, I asked a couple of friends if they noticed that I rarely looked them in the eye. They said they hadn't noticed. Maybe people don't get out from inside their heads to see what others are actually doing.

I grew up with lots of social anxiety, social paranoia. I had trouble talking with people, always felt they didn't like me, always knew they didn't understand me. Always interested in the workings of the mind (why was I so strange and anxious?), I majored in psychology in college and got a Master's degree in experimental social psychology. I was in a Ph.D. program, but left with the Master's because I was expected to create hypotheses about why people behave the way they do, yet I felt I didn't really understand people.

I began working and eventually met an astrologer with whom I became friends. He taught me astrology over a period of years. That really helped me a lot, because it gave me a tool for understanding people. I could mathematically calculate a person's chart and see all the factors in their personality and how those factors interrelated and how they interrelated with me and why people did the things they did. I think I learned more psychology through astrology than I ever did in college. Now I don't calculate charts much anymore, but I've had enough experience reading them that I can understand the various factors that may interrelate to create any given personality — I understand the possibilities.

I dabbled in Tarot for a while, which also helped me. As a child, along with reading people's feelings in their eyes, I felt I could also know what they were thinking. But everyone denied it. That left me really confused. Through reading Tarot, I learned that (1) people will never admit that you know what they're thinking (maybe because it invades their personal space and privacy?) and (2) much of the time people don't even know what they're thinking. The first two cards in the Tarot layout concern the question being asked. When I would read the question from the cards, people would tell me I was wrong, that was not their question. They would deny even thinking about that topic. If I pushed and pushed, they would eventually admit that it was in the back of their mind, but insist that it wasn't relevant. Yet how often does what is in the back of the mind determine what the person expresses? Eventually I quit reading Tarot — too hard to communicate with the people.

I don't know if being able to read people's

thoughts and feelings is AS or not. I only do it to help myself understand people so I could relate better. But that was part of what led me onto a spiritual path in my life. My difficulty in social situations, the anxiety it causes, has led me to lead a very solitary life. I need large amounts of time in solitude to decompress after social interactions. But on the spiritual path, you need to spend a lot of time in solitude in order to progress. Once I realised my need for solitude, I actively pursued it and learned to really enjoy being alone. And of course, that allows me to make brief forays into socialising with others without coming all unglued.

As a child, I sought solitude and silence alone in nature. There was a wooded area near my house where I would often go. Then I started college and later working, and there was no place to be in nature. Eventually, I moved from the large city where I was working to a small alpine town with lots of forest and recreational activities. I started hiking and camping and soon backpacking and Nordic skiing, all alone. It provided great relief from the stresses of my work life.

I have heard that autistic children often relate

better with animals than with humans. I think I understand that. Animals relate in a straightforward manner, not playing games, not pretending to be something they are not, not demanding that you feed their ego or their idea of how you should relate. Humans, on the other hand, are all those things that animals are not. I think humans have a lot to learn about relating in a straightforward manner. They would be a lot less confusing and intimidating that way.

I found social activities with friends just as stressful as interactions on the job. I eventually learned that my breaking point in group activities was around six people. I felt fairly comfortable with up to three people that I knew well. At six, I started to freak out. I didn't like having get-togethers in my home, because it would be rude to suddenly tell the people to leave when I started stressing; at someone else's home or in a public place, I could leave and go home to de-stress.

I retired from work a couple years ago, something I'd looked forward to for a long time. At this point in my life, I can handle most social situations. If I don't feel comfortable, I leave the situation. If people don't like it, too bad, that's how I am.

I don't think that having family and friends and a busy social life are necessarily the greatest things in life or what we all should do. If I have a high IQ and the majority of others have an average IQ, am I to assume they know best? It was hard for me to break away from that mold of following the majority, and that mold is fine for the people who want it, but it's not necessarily the best way. Through spending so much time alone, I've learned to do things myself, and I've gained a great deal of self-confidence and self-assurance that I can provide for, and take care of, myself. I think, especially as a woman, that that is more important than having family or a great social life. I've learned to be comfortable with who I am.

Personal Stories Part 2 — James

My issues with Asperger's started at a young age, although I had no clue that I had Asperger's. I can only hope relating my story will help others understand their situation and overcome its obstacles.

Life was strange, people were hard to relate to. I just didn't 'get it'. I tried too hard to make friends; it didn't work by just trying to let it happen naturally. I was lonely but didn't understand how to make friends. All I wanted was a couple of 'good buddies'. To date I have still not accomplished it.

It was hard to focus in school as I always felt out of place. My parents were no help; they wanted me to be like everyone else but didn't (or wouldn't try to) understand why I wasn't. I couldn't focus and received terrible grades in school (until college, where I could focus on one subject extensively). All I was good at was 'foolin' around'. I was an expert in daydreaming and could space out at will, no matter what was happening around me. Perhaps it was just me escaping an unpleasant existence.

I was/am an adrenaline junkie. I get bored easily and seek out excitement: hang gliding, driving fast cars, sailplanes, race cars and boats, exploring most new activities, meeting new people on a one-to-one basis, etc.

I am great one-on-one with new people but have difficulty in groups of people. I am not very good at chit-chat, but can get deeply involved in single-subject conversations. This has been a hindrance in the working world, where networking & putting yourself 'out there' is a necessary skill. I have failed several times in business and selling positions. Where I excel is in project-orientated tasks.

Ask me to fix something for you or build something, I am right on it with a successful outcome every time. Ask me to convince others to buy something, not so well.

Even now, at 70, I still do have only a couple of friends that are similar enough to me that I like being around them for long periods of time. Even with them I sometimes get this feeling of wanting to escape and get back to my life alone.

I have issues with feeling love for people. I can experience empathy for others though.

Even my children sometimes feel like strangers to me. Although I yearn for a 'family feeling', I don't experience it, even when I'm spending time with my children. For some reason my brother and I have a connection that I don't experience with anyone else.

Since I don't like to waste my time when I could be doing something I would rather be doing, I don't invest the time to just 'hang out' and get to know strangers better. I'm uncomfortable in these situations since it is hard for me to know what to say next or keep the conversation going unless it is a discussion about something specific.

I am an observer and this trait makes people uncomfortable sometimes, because I can be so focused on them. Some people have called me too intense.

To help me make sense of the world I have experimented with psychedelic drugs, astrology, religion, the Law of Attraction and meditation.

Other than the Law of Attraction the most helpful has been Eckhart Tolle's philosophy of 'being here in the now' as much as possible. Eckhart has many YouTube videos you can view for free.

Listening to my intuition as a guide when I get to a dead end and seeking to shut off the constant chatter of my brain so I can think clearly and stay in the present has been very helpful.

As a result of my not understanding the cause of my difficulties (I didn't take the free online Asperger's Test on this website until last year), I have been through 5 marriages/divorces, 4 failed businesses, and have spent 50% of my life living alone. Asperger's has not been an easy life to live.

My favourite affirmation: stepping outside your comfort box makes your comfort box bigger.

Just knowing why I was having a difficult way in the world has made a major difference in my life. I am more confident in social situations, more confident in my ability to manage life, and more satisfied with my life. I am actually experiencing happiness and gratitude on a daily basis ... not something that was part of my normal existence.

James

Personal Stories Part 3 — Marie

I happened to do the Aspie test on your site in 2012, and two other times since then.

And my score was always around 32/33 — confirmed Aspie!

In fact, I was more relieved than desperate; I was even grateful for the life I had in spite of many difficulties. I am grateful because, unlike many children today, I have never been officially diagnosed, so even if I saw many books about "how to raise a difficult child" on my mother's table, I just grew up trying to find my own way and I recognised how my two parents were both naturally gifted to raise a "difficult child" like I was.

It certainly was helpful for me to grow in normality WITH my own difference. I always felt I was 'different': I had lots of motricity difficulties — my eyes were not straight, I was a silent observer, living in an ivory tower, drawing a lot. I asked so many questions in school that the teacher told my mom to keep me home at one stage because she was just so exhausted by my many questions. But instead of punishing me, my mother taught me to draw on the big papers she placed on my room walls.

In school I was often bullied and I felt I had no defence, but I always found nice girls who were older and mature and they lent me good books so I became very good at writing stories.

Later, I became a high school teacher, teaching grades 8 and 12 in French and Ethics. My methods were different and I was able to give each pupil his/her place and value their talents and skills. I also worked a lot to improve my own skills and undertook many courses and therapies. I wanted to get over my own difficulties, which were like an invisible handicap. What helped me the most was my ability to recognise others' skills and talents, and to value them in each student.

But it took me so much of my energy that I simply didn't have room for having a family; I needed so much time just to relax and be myself that I needed all my private time for rest as well as for my preparations.

I had very few friends, but solid ones. They never did reject me. Then after 12 years in teaching high school, I earned a Master's degree in my free time and I was hired at university level, and there, during my working years, I got my Doctorate degree. The miracle was that I was under contract (no tenure), near 25 years working full time but with the opportunity to organise my time; this was an approach valuing results more than the number of hours at my office. So I was able to organise my time between being physically present with the students (I was a field education director) and all the other necessities of such a task, giving myself the time and space needed to be able to cope with my handicap.

Today I am retired and it is the best time of my life, not only because I live with a nice pension plan, but because I spent all my life without a name on my secret handicaps. I just learned how to cope WITH them on an everyday basis and it is only since I've retired that I have come to realise, through your website, that the problem all along was that I had Asperger's Syndrome! Imagine!

Through doing everything possible during my whole life to manage my condition, I became a quiet and contemplative person devoted to her students and even low profile with my university peers. I am grateful that they recognised and valued my work and I only got good help from them when needed and lots of respect and mutuality for encouraging the students to see what is possible.

I will soon turn 65 and I am grateful to be able to live WITH who I became along the way and I don't wish to get a formal diagnosis from a psychiatric hospital to certify the type of Autism I was born with.

I wish I could simply have some opportunities to volunteer my time to help autistic children and their parents, in order to share joys and hopes by encouraging them to accept their situation and work through it for the best.

Sincerely yours and long life to your website!

Marie

Personal Stories Part 4 — Robert

Some people are born feeling different. One of my earliest memories is of being at playgroup (or kindergarten, as you may well now call it), sitting having milk with all the other kids in the class, hearing the general hubbub around about me and knowing, somehow, that I was not, for some reason, part of it.

I would never want to, or be willing to, join in with class activities, would clam up when fellow pupils (and also teachers) got too close to me, would start to cry and, in at least two cases I can remember, had a complete breakdown in the classroom. When asked why I had done so, I could never ever explain why this had happened. I did not, it seems, know right from wrong.

A classic example of this was the playground in Primary One. I was on a high, nervous or excited about something or other (I can't remember what). Everyone else in the playground was either lining up all neatly and politely, in preparation for going into class, or else was quietly gathering in small groups, chatting to each other. I, on the other hand, was alone, in the middle of the playground. Laughing and chatting away to myself, I was shouting out to anyone who happened to pass. Mainly, at that time of the morning, it was teachers. I remember the prefects coming over and shouting at me, telling me to behave and be quiet.

Another memory from that time. My class running around in the gym. Doing so until the teacher told us to stop. I did not understand what we were being told to do. Either that or I got so carried away in the moment that I just forgot to stop. Another row from the teacher and another case of me not knowing why I was in the wrong.

And one last final example from my early schooldays. One that, even now, still sticks very sorely in my mind's eye. A group of kids in the playground, playing some kind of gang or group game. It might have been tig (or he, or whatever you call it now). They were all shouting and whooping (as normal kids do when they are in a group) and I did not know why. I had no guidance, no-one there to explain things to me. In fear and haste, I lashed out and hit the one nearest to me. Hauled up by the teacher, I was asked by her if I felt that what I had done was necessary. Now, I had previously been told by my parents that it is wrong to lie. So, when asked, I said yes.

Here is the crux of the matter – I did not realise that what I had done was wrong and did not want to appear stupid by asking. I am sure that parents and Asperger's 'sufferers' (a term which I deliberately use here in inverted commas) will both relate to the situation I speak of here. That which, from the one side, is frustrating because you, as a parent, have explained to your child time and again why saying or doing a particular thing is wrong and you cannot understand why they say yes, seeming to understand then go off and do exactly the same thing again and you are banging your head against a brick wall because you do not know what else to do to get through to them.

Then, on the other hand, if you are an Asperger's 'sufferer', you know that you have done something which you should not have done, quite possibly again, yet you have no idea either why it is wrong or what you could possibly have done to avoid it. You have not seen the signs which 'everyone else' can plainly see.

That was what life was like for me growing up. Yes, there were (and still are) lots of happy times to be had but there were (and sometimes still are) many times of anxiety, doubt and worry simply because I don't know what the hell I am supposed to be doing.

Much as my parents loved me, they were almost always at the end of their tether with me. I could not walk or run as fast as 'everyone else'. I could not do simple things such as tie my shoelaces, climb over a stile or tie up a pair of skipping ropes without having every such task broken down for me into the smallest possible steps. This was done once with a smile, twice with a scream and thrice with a resigned sigh and an "I've told you so" look. Looking back now, I have the greatest admiration and respect for my parents and the way they handled me. It cannot have been easy for them, both working full time and then having to come home and explain the same things time and again to a child who just did not seem to take anything else on board. Everyone else around about them was having babies; none of them were having these problems, so I suppose none of them could relate to what my mum and dad were going through.

And so, the question arises, when did I realise I was different from others? Well, there have been a few signposts along the way. The first ones I have already discussed, but there were some new ones awaiting me in my teenage years. As my mum often said to me then, you can't remain a baby all your life.

That was not what I wanted at all. Only, I did not know how to express this. I didn't know how to change. I didn't know how to adapt. I didn't know how others felt. I didn't know why the same things kept happening. I didn't know why I was different. I just knew that I was. A case in point — my first successful job interview. An Edinburgh shoe shop ... I was told I had nice manners. I was told I came across very well. Then I was let loose on the shop floor. My first customer ... I guided them to a more experienced colleague, as I had been instructed to do, told the colleague what the customer wanted and then left the two of them to it. I went back to tidying the shoes, as I had been instructed to do when it was quiet.

My manager approached me, asked what I was doing. I explained what I had done. The exchange then went a bit like this:

Manager: Robert (short and deadly sigh) who is the most important person in the shop?

Me: (sweating and thinking fast) Er, the customer?

Manager: That's right, so why are you not serving them? You should have followed their request right through, not just palmed them off onto your colleague, shouldn't you?

Me: (looking crestfallen) Yes, I'm very sorry. It won't happen again.

Only it did, two days later. I had to serve some customers with kids. I was so nervous I forgot to ask for the shoe size. The kid wouldn't sit still. I had 100 things to think about at once. I couldn't do it. I didn't know why. I tried my very best. Sweat was pouring off me and I was in tears. Could I not get anything right? After an eternity, my manager pulled me up, gave me my coat and told me to just leave. Two things she said to me still stick in my mind to this day.

"Your problem, Robert, is that you seem to lack any common sense."

"That last serving should have taken seconds."

Oh, for sure, there were plenty of experts around afterwards, telling me what I should have done, why I shouldn't have frozen; honestly it was so simple, why could I not have just done it? Everyone else would have dealt with it in half the time; why could I not just get a grip on things and bloody well do them properly? And at that point (this is where it gets really good) I didn't know I had Asperger's Syndrome, so even I didn't know what the hell was wrong with me.

The advice I have been given by many people (family, friends, close and otherwise) in the twenty years which have followed the scene described has sometimes been a help and sometimes been a hindrance. Only sometimes, in retrospect, have I been able to work out which it was. And this is where I will start to wind down.

These are, in part, the experiences that have helped form me into who I am today and they continue to burn into my brain and cause me to stand up for myself and others in a similar position. So, here, for what it is worth, is what I have learned from my life with Asperger's so far.

What advice was I given?

Watch what you're saying to people. This nugget will crop up time and again in your formative years and you have to take it on board if you want your social skills to improve.

You just have to accept that.

This, again, will recur regularly, especially if whoever it is around you who is giving it either does not know that you have Asperger's Syndrome or is bullying you. It will also come from parents and carers who will be tired and stressed from what they see as incessant questioning and unnecessary problems caused by you not listening or "for some reason" just not doing what is asked of you or expected of you. Put yourself in their position. They won't necessarily know of, or be able to identify with, the problems you are having. They won't understand why you have or have not done something in a particular way. Try and explain to them why this has happened. Don't be ashamed of having Asperger's Syndrome because it's not your fault you've got it. Take a deep breath, step back from the situation, work out what went wrong and why and then, when things have calmed down, discuss this with your parents.

And parents — the same goes for you!

Try seeing things from your kids' points of view. Don't make every wee word or wee chat with them a list of don'ts, tempting though it may be. Look out for signs of stress or discomfort in your kids. Don't scream or shout at them in the heat of the moment, because that's just going to make things worse. Watch how you phrase the advice or help you share with them. Admit both to them and to yourselves when you have made a mistake. Share your feelings, both good and bad, with them as this will create a bind of honesty that will cement an understanding between you. Remember that they are not everybody else's kids and that some families are just far better than others at shielding problems and tensions. Be as approachable to them as you would wish others to be to you. Never assume that they have done, or would do, something just because it is "the sort of stupid thing that they would do". Imagine how you would feel if people got stressed out at you or had a go at you, seemingly without reason.

Encourage your kids to speak openly and honestly ... about their feelings and experiences in an appropriate setting. Go that extra mile and teach them what sarcasm, jealousy and bullying looks and sounds like. With your love and help and support, through both good times and bad, they will gain the tools for a successful and happy life and the wisdom with which to use them.

That is what my parents have taught me and what and what I now feel duty-bound to pass on to you.

Personal Stories Part 5 — Darren

I hear it probably 10,000 times per year. The applause, the shouts of joy, the desire to have me back soon.

Twenty years ago, what I heard 10,000 times per year was the derision, the torment, the ostracism.

What a difference information and time make!

My name is Darren Lambert and I have Autism. I was diagnosed with Asperger's syndrome in 2012, at age 32. To say that life is often very difficult for a person with Autism is an understatement, and I doubt I need to explain why. However, one can have Autism and a tough childhood in addition, and still end up as a happy, fulfilled adult doing something that you'd never expect to see an autistic person do!

My wife and I are musical entertainers. That one single sentence carries a lot of hope for people with Autism! Let's pick it apart.

I am happily married and I have been for four years now. My wife is neurotypical, and with what

we do for a living, we're with each other all the
time, with very few exceptions. I am considered
'high-functioning autistic' and any autistic
person's mind will be substantially different from
the mind of a neurotypical person. Yet, that has
not caused us any significant trouble, nor has
being around each other constantly for four years.
The sheer number of articles that you can find
when searching the Internet for "Can marriage
work if you're autistic?" shows that it is a question
frequently asked, in silence if not audibly, by
many people. The simple answer is a resounding
"YES!"... and there's not much to it!

Like most people with Asperger's, I am unusually
gifted in mathematics. My wife is not gifted in that
area. Therefore, whenever anything mathematical
needs to be done, I do it. However, like many
people with Asperger's, my mind is constantly
racing with thoughts. This makes me oblivious to
a lot of what goes on around me. My wife, on the
other hand, is the most observant person I know,
and she has a memory that still amazes me to this
day. So whenever we need to recall or remember
something, that's her domain. She's the emotional
thinker, I'm the logical thinker. It's understood
that whatever we do must make sense, but each of

us brings a perspective to the table that the other one often didn't consider at first. Our mental differences are aligned such that what each of us lacks, the other provides. If that condition is achieved in a relationship between an autistic person and a neurotypical person, it works very easily indeed. Beyond that, we share just about all of the same interests and desires, so we have everything else that a good marriage should have, and I believe that "until death do us part" will be a happy journey indeed!

The autistic person can leverage his or her autistic qualities as positives rather than negatives. Often, young autistic people feel like they have some extremely unusual traits or desires; perhaps so extreme that those traits or desires could never be "loved" by another person. If there is one thing to be gathered from this part of my story, it's that that is an entirely untrue statement! My wife may never share, for instance, my fixation on the design of the speedometer in vehicles I view, but it sure has given rise to its share of jokes ... and when you both get a laugh, your bond strengthens and your life lengthens! There's nothing not to love about that.

It might be easy enough to imagine how a neurotypical person can be an entertainer, but, surprisingly, it's just as easy — if not easier — to see how an autistic person can be an entertainer! Autistic people frequently feel like fish out of water when they are in group settings. I know that feeling all too well. I still have difficulty navigating the waters of social interaction and I am almost 35 years old. I feel awkward in groups when I am "mingling", largely because I know from experience how unlikely it is that I will encounter someone with whom I have enough in common to sustain a conversation that goes beyond shallow platitudes. Furthermore, I find the "rules of socialisation" to be nebulous and almost impossible to comprehend in a concrete fashion. If I do find someone with whom I can have a conversation, usually I converse with that person one-on-one, as possible, even if the others in the group are nearby. I simply tune out everything that everyone else is saying around me. It's not uncommon that I will retreat to a place of solitude after two or three hours of being in a group of people, because I've simply had enough — it does take effort to tune out the sensory chaos of group interaction for a long time. This is something I doubt I will ever be able to change, and there's no way that I'm the only one who feels like that.

However, one main reason why I'm writing this story is to give autistic people, and those who love them, hope. There is hope for an autistic person to become comfortable in a group setting. I have achieved this. 500 times per year, I get up in front of groups of people, ranging from a dozen to hundreds, and entertain them. By being an entertainer, I control the group. When I'm singing and/or playing, they're listening. When I'm telling a story or a joke, they're listening. If someone says anything, it's usually only one or two people at a time and I can easily converse with them briefly on the microphone while everyone else listens. If I am in control of the group, I am essentially setting the rules, so the situation becomes logical and understandable. There's no sensory chaos when I'm doing a song ... and if it should ever happen, I can turn the volume up — which drowns it out and encourages it to effectively stop!

For a long time, I thought that I would never be comfortable with groups of people. I can still hear, in my "mind's ear", one of my 7th-grade teachers constantly telling me to "blend", in a stern voice.

I've never been able to blend in with my peers and I know that many autistic people I've encountered have felt the same way. What that teacher should have told me was "lead". The autistic person is well-suited to be a leader, because leaders make the rules and call the shots, and their tendency to think logically makes them unusually well-equipped to create the structure of a situation. I know that once I became a leader and recognised that I was far better suited to leading than blending, I felt like I had found my niche. These days I am around groups constantly and I feel no awkwardness at all.

In my younger years, from age 10 through to almost age 16, I would wake up dreading almost every day when I had to go to school. If I had to go to school, I didn't even want to get out of bed. I would regularly cry on Sunday nights, knowing that I had another week of school ahead of me … largely because I knew what I would experience at the hands of the people I would encounter.

Often, the high-functioning autistic feels like he/she is trapped inside his/her own body. There are desires to do unusual things, but the feeling is that if those desires are manifested observably, they could generate ridicule or at least exhortations to do something different. The thing is — we don't want to do something different! For example, I used to like listening to the same song over and over on repeat play, sometimes several dozen times in a row. That drove people crazy! But I didn't want to listen to any other song. It was like a mental itch that begged to be scratched. Sometimes you scratch an itch and it comes back repeatedly! To this day I still sometimes listen to certain songs on repeat play.

It's very important for an autistic person to be given a lot of freedom with activities and pursuits as long as those pursuits are not harmful, starting from a very young age, even if watching the person indulge in such fills your mind with questions. You never know what might become of it! For me, all of those years of listening to various songs over and over have indelibly etched the nuances of the songs into my mind, and now when I perform them live, I can provide a very accurate replication of the songs for my audiences. Recently, my wife and I performed a song that I used to listen to, over and over, in my junior year of high school. (After that, I'd only heard it maybe two or three times per year on the radio.) 18 years later, Kristen and I were asked to do that same song at a show. We had never performed nor practised the song. She found the lyrics, I set up my keyboards for the accompaniment ... and we pulled it off near-perfectly! Largely due to how many times I listened to that song in my teens, I knew what the accompaniment notes and chords were, what instrument sounds to use and where, and even what, the vocal harmony notes were! Who'd have thought?

Fast-forward 20 years ... now I never wake up dreading what I do, no matter how many shows we are to perform that day. I look forward to what I am going to experience at the hands of the people I will encounter! Recently, a lady who heard our show told me, "You must sleep really well at night!" — and it wasn't because she thought I would be tired after having done a show! She said that I seemed really happy, and as such I would be likely to be able to sleep well at night, and she was right. People with Asperger's often tend to be unusually gifted in music should they pursue it, and I have managed to parlay that gift into a very fulfilling career. The fact that I get to do it with the woman I love makes it many times better.

If I had been aware of my condition in my middle-school years and had been given the opportunity at that time to switch it out and become neurotypical, I would have taken that opportunity in a heartbeat. Now that I have found a perfect fit for the way I am, I wouldn't even dream of changing it. Autistic people CAN make a life that is energizing and fulfilling for themselves, even in a world that is geared toward the neurotypical population majority. This may have to be achieved in an unusual way, and that should be encouraged as often as possible. Too often was I encouraged to pursue a life I might best describe as 'conventional' when nobody knew I was autistic, and though I did try that in a few different ways, it never worked. I felt like a square block trying to shove myself into a round hole. The simplest advice I could give to another autistic person comes in two short sentences — "Be true to yourself" and "Be unconventional". The closer I've adhered to those axioms, the happier I've been. Find that square hole. Because, after all, though most of the 'blocks' out there are 'round', not one of them will fit into it!

Conclusion

I hope you have found this book helpful and could relate to some of the real life stories.

I know that the journey involved with having Asperger's Syndrome is not always an easy one. What is important is that you don't give yourself a hard time. Accept yourself for who you are and for the gifts you have. You cannot be anybody else. However, at the same time, never give up on your dreams and thereby feel limited by Asperger's Syndrome. Many things in our lives that we think are not possible actually are.

If you enjoyed the book, I would really appreciate it if you could give us a good review on Amazon. It really helps to reach more people and spread the awareness.

If you would like to receive more information from the Asperger's Test Site, including useful tips and interesting articles about Asperger's, you can sign up to our email list at http://www.aspergerstestsite.com/newsletter.

If you are interested in learning more about the emotional aspects of Asperger's Syndrome, including dealing with stress, anxiety and depression, I highly recommend you check out my other book, "Emotional Mastery for adults with Asperger's", available on Amazon at: http://amzn.to/1LMyCf7.

All the best

Mark

Thank you and Acknowledgements

This book would not have been possible without the words of support I have received from readers of the <u>Asperger's Test Site</u>. So I would firstly like to thank all of you for supporting the site and the project over the years. Without such small words of gratitude and encouragement, I would have given up on the project.

The comments you have left on many of the articles have also served to inspire others on their journey of self-discovery. What started out as an information site has quickly become a community where you all help each other.

Next, I would like to thank all of the people who contributed an article, to both this book and the website. It is amazing to have different perspectives of your experiences of living with Asperger's and the diversity of nationalities and age ranges. It has certainly helped to increase the quality of information provided by this book.

I would like to thank Darren Lambert for his help in proofing and reviewing this book and educating me on the differences between US and UK English.

And last but not least, I would really like to thank and appreciate Kym Holwerda, who has become the Aspergers Test Site's proof reader. Kym offered her support to the site in May 2014, at a time when I was really struggling to stay on top of things. She provides valuable insights into the articles we publish and has so diligently edited all of the articles published on the site. My grammar and spelling are not always the best in the world, so I feel immensely grateful to have her on the team. I have felt immense support from her with both the website and the writing of this book. She has thoroughly proof read this book and educated me in the subtle differences between US and UK English. I know many of you are triggered by the spelling and grammar used on the site and have confused UK English for bad grammar and spelling, but Kym is English, as am I (although she now lives in Australia).

Made in the USA
San Bernardino, CA
27 February 2017